THE ANGLO-IRISH TRADITION

by the same author

—

THE MAKING OF MODERN IRELAND

CONFRONTATIONS: STUDIES IN IRISH HISTORY

THE
ANGLO-IRISH TRADITION

J. C. BECKETT

Cornell University Press

ITHACA, NEW YORK

First published in 1976

International Standard Book Number 0–8014–1056–8
Library of Congress Catalog Card Number 76–20093

Printed in Great Britain by Ebenezer Baylis and Son Ltd. The Trinity Press, Worcester, and London

77–04799

Contents

Preface

This book, a work of reflection rather than of research, was written in fulfilment of a resolve made more than thirty years ago. During that long interval my ideas on the subject have undergone many changes; but my belief in the importance of the Anglo-Irish tradition remains unshaken.

Once again, as on similar occasions in the past, I must acknowledge my indebtedness to Mr. J. L. Lord, to whose encouragement and criticism I owe more than I can well express.

October 1975.   J. C. Beckett

Prologue

On Tuesday, 16 April 1782, the streets of Dublin were filled with excited but orderly crowds. Parliament was about to meet; and the Patriot leader, Henry Grattan, was to make there a Declaration of Rights—less radical than the American Declaration of a few years earlier, but breathing the same spirit of national independence. In Dublin, and throughout Ireland, men's minds were turned to College Green and the great event so soon to take place there.

At five o'clock in the afternoon the Speaker took the chair. The House was full. The galleries were crowded. The necessary preliminaries took little time. Then Grattan rose in his place, amid an air of hushed expectancy: the famous orator was now to enshrine in immortal language the national claim, of whose victory everyone already felt assured. Nor did Grattan disappoint his hearers: his speech, one of the greatest of his whole career, displayed to the full that splendour of language and fertility of imagination for which he was famous:

> I am now to address a free people. Ages have passed away, and this is the first moment in which you could be distinguished by that appellation. I have spoken on the subject of your liberty so often that I have nothing to add, and have only to admire by what heaven-directed steps you have proceeded until the whole faculty of the nation is braced up to the act of her own deliverance. I found Ireland on her knees. I watched over her with an eternal solicitude. I have traced her progress from injuries to arms, and from arms to liberty. Spirit of Swift, spirit of Molyneux, your genius has prevailed. Ireland is now a nation. In that new character I hail her, and bowing to her august presence I say, *Esto perpetua.*

One short sentence from this, the most famous passage in the speech, contains the essence of what Grattan had to say: 'Ireland is now a nation.' The whole assembly was already convinced of the truth of this assertion; but to hear it solemnly pronounced by the man whom they regarded as the father of his country gave it a new force, a new reality. Without a division, without a dissentient voice, the whole House joined

9

with Grattan in assuring King George III that 'his subjects of Ireland are a free people'.

'Ireland is now a nation': to men of a later age it has seemed a strange assertion in that place and at that time. The House of Commons that Grattan addressed was composed of Protestant gentry, Protestant lawyers, Protestant merchants. On his way to the parliament house that afternoon he had passed through streets lined by armed Volunteers, drawn from all ranks of the Protestant community. Roman Catholics formed the great bulk of the population; yet no Catholic could sit in parliament, or vote, or hold office under the crown, or bear arms. If Ireland was indeed a nation, it was a nation in which a Protestant minority had a monopoly of power, while a Catholic majority sat, as it were, on the fringes of the constitution, free to live and worship, to trade and make money, but carefully excluded from any share in the government of the country.

It is to the citizens of this 'Protestant nation', and their descendants, that we commonly give the name 'Anglo-Irish'. It is essentially a historian's term. Grattan and his Protestant contemporaries never doubted that they were Irishmen, without any qualification. Though they were, for the most part, of English descent and loyal to the English crown, it did not occur to them to suppose that they could, on that account, be regarded as less than Irish, or that their claim to represent the Irish nation could be denied. But by the time of Grattan's death, in 1820, a shift of opinion was already evident; and it became more sharply marked during the next generation. The change was noted by one of the powerful Beresford family, which had dominated much of Irish political life in the later eighteenth century. 'When I was a boy', he said, ' "the Irish people" meant the Protestants; now it means the Roman Catholics.' A Protestant might still be an Irishman; but he was on the way to becoming an Irishman with a difference.

The Gaelic revival of the later nineteenth century sharpened the sense of national distinctiveness and gave it a new quality. To be truly Irish now meant to be Gaelic; and any other claim to 'Irishness' must be in some way qualified. It was in response to this narrower and more exclusive nationalism that the term 'Anglo-Irish' came into use; though it can be found much earlier, in various contexts, it was only at this time that it acquired general currency. If the term were to be strictly interpreted, it would have to be applied to almost every aspect of Irish life. There is very little in Ireland—from the way people are governed to the food they eat and the language they speak—that does not reveal the dominant influence of England. But such an honest application would rob the term of any distinctive force and thus foil its essential purpose, which is to pick out one section of the population as less truly 'Irish' than the rest. 'Anglo-Irish', in ordinary usage, denotes the Protestant community that dominated Ireland in the eighteenth century and those who inherited and maintained its tradition in the changed and changing circumstances of a later age. It is in this sense that the term is used here. But it is used merely for convenience, without any of the apologetic connotation that it may seem to imply; and its use is not to be regarded as any concession to the racialism prevalent in a good deal of contemporary Irish thinking. The people with whom we are here concerned are in truth Irish, without any hyphenated prefix; and the fact that they must be distinguished by some special term simply reflects the unhealed divisions of Ireland, past and present. The Anglo-Irish are, in Yeats's famous phrase, 'no petty people'; and Ireland without them would be not only a different but a poorer country.

It is customary to think of the Anglo-Irish of the eighteenth century as the descendants of recent settlers, established in the country by the Stuarts and by Cromwell, and separated from the earlier population by race no less than by religion. There is much truth in this, but not the whole truth. We shall misunderstand the Anglo-Irish completely unless we remember that they represent something more than the final layers in a process of colonization that had been going on since the twelfth century. The Ireland into which the seventeenth-century settlers had come was not a Gaelic Ireland. It was an Ireland already dominated by English institutions and English traditions. The armies that Cromwell met and defeated did not fight in the name of Irish independence, but in the name of King Charles II; and they were led by James Butler, Marquess of Ormond, whose ancestors had come to Ireland in the twelfth century. In comparison with Ormond and a great part of those who fought under his command, the settlers who followed in the wake of the Cromwellian conquest were 'new men'; but they were also the heirs of five centuries of colonial history. The tradition that they and their descendants developed was shaped by their own experience and the circumstances of their own time; but its roots ran deep into the Irish past, far beyond the wars and conquests of the seventeenth century to a little band of Anglo-Norman adventurers who arrived in Ireland in the reign of Henry II to establish England's first colony.

I

England's Oldest Colony

At the creek of Baginbun
Ireland was lost and won.

Baginbun Head is a bold promontory, stretching out into the Irish Sea from the southern coast of County Wexford. Before the days of light-houses and lightships it was a coast notoriously dangerous to shipping; but Baginbun Head, with a subsidiary projection running at right angles to the main promontory, provides a cove or creek where vessels may be sheltered from the waves, and where access to the land is, if not easy, at least practicable. Here landed, on 1 May 1169, Maurice Prendergast, Hervey de Montmorency and Robert FitzStephen, with three shiploads of their followers—'ninety heroes dressed in mail', say the Irish annals, adding, curiously enough, 'and the Gaels set little store by them'. It was a fatal misjudgement, for these were the men who were to lay the first foundations of English power in Ireland.

The men themselves would hardly seem, in our eyes, to be English at all. They were a mixture of Anglo-Norman and Welsh, with, possibly, a few Flemings; and their language, at least the language of their leaders, was French. But they were all subjects of the king of England, Henry II; their expedition was made, if not under his direct authority, at least with his permission; contemporary writers habitually describe them as Englishmen and, at least on occasion, this was how they described them-selves. Whatever their race or nationality, they were certainly English in a political sense; and they were the forerunners of an English settle-ment that was to exercise a decisive influence on the course of Irish history.

They had not come to Ireland on any chance raid or mere freebooting expedition, nor were they the spearhead of an aggressive foreign invasion. They came because they had been invited by the king of Leinster, in whose territories they landed. This king, Dermot MacMurrough, being hard pressed in a war with his own subjects, had received permission from Henry II to recruit forces in South Wales; and Maurice Prendergast

13

and his companions were the first of these allies to arrive. Once the news reached MacMurrough, who had been holding out stubbornly in hope of relief, he marched to join them. Ninety men might not seem to make much difference; but these were men whose daring, skill and superior equipment put new courage into MacMurrough's scanty forces and overawed his enemies. Before very long he was in control of his kingdom again.

But this success aroused MacMurrough's ambition. He was no longer satisfied with Leinster and hoped that further help from abroad would enable him to extend his territories. During his recruiting tour in South Wales he had negotiated with a powerful magnate, Richard de Clare, better known in Irish history as 'Strongbow', and had tried to secure his services by the offer of his daughter Eva in marriage and, with her, the succession to the kingdom of Leinster. Now he renewed the offer, holding out, this time, the prospect of subduing all Ireland. Though Strongbow had been dilatory in responding to the earlier offer, he now determined to act and to throw all his resources into the venture. But many months were consumed in the necessary preparations; and it was not until August 1170 that he landed near Waterford, with two hundred knights and some thousands of more lightly armed troops. By this time MacMurrough's subjects were once again in revolt; and now they had secured the aid of his bitterest enemy, Rory O'Connor, king of Connaught, who was also High King of Ireland—a title of some honour, but conveying no more practical authority than the holder could impose by force of arms. Even with the powerful reinforcements that Strongbow had brought, it took a year's hard fighting to crush rebellion in Leinster, to humble O'Connor and to drive away the Norsemen whom he had called in from the Isle of Man to assist his cause. But by the summer of 1171 the task was at length completed. In the interval, MacMurrough himself had died; and Strongbow, on the strength of his marriage with Eva, had taken possession of Leinster. But he knew well that things could not rest there. Henry II would never tolerate the establishment of an independent Norman state on his western flank; and the new king of Leinster lost no time in trying to persuade his sovereign that he was still a loyal subject.

Henry had, in fact, been watching the course of events with growing anxiety. Already he was collecting troops and material for an expedition to Ireland that would be strong enough to convince his adventurous vassals that he was still their master. He was not to be deflected from his purpose by Strongbow's assurance of his loyalty and readiness to do homage for Leinster. The preparations went steadily forward; and on 16 October 1171 Henry set sail from Pembroke, with a large fleet conveying some five hundred knights and three or four thousand archers, with all the stores and equipment needed for an extended campaign. Next day, he landed at Crook, near Waterford. Here Strongbow met him and surrendered the city into his hands. He was, however, allowed to keep Leinster, for which he did homage to the king.

Once these arrangements had been completed Henry did not linger long in Waterford. He realized that Dublin, though far inferior as a port, was of major strategic importance; and it was at Dublin that he took up his residence in a wooden palace built for him on the outskirts of the city. Here he held his court, from November to March. In later centuries this was to be the period of the 'Castle season', when Dublin society gave dinners and balls and made a gay show at viceregal levees within a few hundred yards of the spot where the first English king to assert his authority over Ireland had received and entertained his new subjects. The coincidence of dates is a mere chance; but there is a genuine line of continuity none the less. From Henry's time onwards, Dublin was the centre of English influence in Ireland, the visible token of a link between the two countries; and even today, when English power has receded and Dublin has become the capital of an Irish republic, it remains the most English city in Ireland.

Henry's stay in Dublin was marked by bustle and activity. The Irish kings, each accompanied by a band of retainers appropriate to his own idea of his importance, flocked to see this mighty potentate, whose dominions stretched from the Pyrenees to the North Sea, to eat strange dishes at his table and to marvel at the splendour of his court. In appearance, at least, all was peace and contentment. Henry's troops kept careful guard, but they were never called upon to fight; and the siege-trains he had so carefully prepared lay idle. The Normans received him as liegemen should receive their lord. The Irish kings made no trouble about swearing fealty. The clergy welcomed him with eager enthusiasm and looked forward to his help in strengthening the discipline of the church. All the arrangements he laid down for the future management of affairs were accepted without question. When he sailed from Wexford on 17 April 1172 this latest addition to his vast empire seemed peaceful and secure.

Henry's plan for Ireland, set out in principle during his visit, was given formal expression in a treaty with Rory O'Connor, made at Windsor a few years later. O'Connor recognized Henry as 'lord of Ireland'; and

Henry confirmed O'Connor in his position as king of Connaught and as High King. In return, O'Connor was to pay tribute for Connaught and to collect, on Henry's behalf, tribute from the other Irish kings. But this arrangement did not include the territory occupied by the Normans. Dublin, Waterford and Wexford the king retained in his own hands; Leinster he had granted to Strongbow and Meath to another Norman magnate, Hugh de Lacy. Ireland was thus partitioned. The lordship embraced the whole country; but part of it was to be governed by feudal law, part by native kings whose subordinate status was indicated by their payment of tribute. The arrangement was perhaps the best that Henry could make in the circumstances; but events were soon to show that it provided no foundation for a lasting peace.

(2)

The connection between Ireland and England thus established has commonly been described as an 'English conquest'; and Irish historians have often seen the whole affair as a typical example of English imperialism, exercised against a weak and peaceful neighbour. There was, in fact, no conquest; and the origins of the connection are to be found in Irish disunity, not in English aggression. Many years earlier, Henry had had before him a proposal for the subjugation of Ireland, put forward by leading English churchmen with the strong backing of the pope. They all urged upon him the pious duty of subduing the Irish, so that they might be rescued from the semi-pagan darkness in which they were believed to dwell and brought into the full light of the gospel as expounded at Rome and Canterbury. It is doubtful if Henry took the proposal seriously; what is certain is that he rejected it. His very different attitude in 1171 did not betoken any change of heart, but a change of circumstances. He had no inclination to be a missionary; and the addition of an outlying province to his straggling and troublesome empire would be a poor return for the expenditure involved in conquering it. But the possibility of an independent Norman principality just across the Irish Sea, in dangerous proximity to Wales, presented a danger that he could not ignore; and it was to counter this danger that he undertook his expedition to Ireland. The forces he carried with him were intended to overawe Strongbow and his companions, not to conquer Ireland; siege-trains would have served little purpose in a war with the natives, who possessed neither castles nor fortified towns. He proclaimed his 'lordship' over the whole country because, in the circumstances of the age, this was the easiest and most obvious way of ensuring some measure of control over future Norman activity; but there is no reason to suppose that he would have interfered in Ireland at all had not his adventurous subjects preceded him and established their power so successfully. And the Norman presence in Ireland can be traced directly to the internal condition of the country and the rival ambitions of Irish kings.

All this may seem remote, of no more than academic interest: since the Normans did settle in Ireland, does the original reason for their coming make any difference? The answer to this question must be that it did make a difference, all the difference in the world. The future of the Norman settlement did not depend only on the character of the Normans themselves but also on the character of the country and the society into which they came; and the character of twelfth-century Ireland has exerted a continuing influence on the history of the country, an influence whose effect is not, even yet, exhausted.

In the twelfth century, Ireland lay on the very fringe of Europe, politically no less than geographically. It can hardly be said, indeed, to have formed any part of the European political system: a European ruler, counting up possible friends or enemies, felt no need to include Ireland in his calculations. It was not a question of natural resources or of geographical position. Norway, a poorer and less fertile country and equally remote from the main centres of power, had its place in the international scene. Ireland was unregarded because it lacked any political machinery through which it could take corporate action. No king, no council, no assembly could negotiate on Ireland's behalf with a foreign power, make a treaty binding on the whole country, or assemble and direct a national army. Yet no country in Europe had had a fairer opportunity of finding its own way to political unity. During the century and a half before the coming of the Normans Ireland had been free from external attack. It was a period during which other countries were achieving some measure of national solidarity and building up institutions —weak and clumsy, very often, but capable of growth—through which an effective central administration could gradually develop. But Irishmen, living apart in a world of their own, made no attempt to follow this pattern; and Ireland remained, as it had been for centuries, no more than a congeries of independent kingdoms, often at war with one another, under a High King, whose authority when he could exert it at all stretched no further than a right to collect tribute. A common language and a common cultural tradition provided the basis for a sense of national distinctiveness; but there was no tradition of common action, nor any machinery for organizing it. Ireland, in fact, was not a state in the contemporary European sense. Had Irishmen possessed the same degree of national solidarity as the Scots had already attained, the Norman settlers would have been absorbed or expelled; and Henry's lordship, had he established it at all, would have proved as transient as his suzerainty over Scotland.

This contrast with Scotland is instructive. During the whole period of their struggle with England the Scots fought for national independence, for a Scottish kingdom under a Scottish king. They were often divided among themselves. There were those of them who were ready to seek English help and acknowledge English superiority. But, through it all, the tradition of a united Scottish nation survived: Scotland had once been an independent kingdom among the kingdoms of Europe, and could be so again. The Ireland to which the Normans came had no such tradition. It was easy for the Irish kings to swear fealty to Henry, because their idea of independence was local, not national; and it did not occur to them that submission to this foreigner could make any difference to their authority within their own territories. Provided they were left in peace, did it matter who claimed to exercise a nominal supremacy over the whole country, or by what title? It is significant of their attitude that they allowed the High Kingship to lapse with the death of Rory O'Connor. It had never been an effective unifying force; but with its passing the only possible rallying centre for a war of independence had gone.

This state of affairs is reflected in the confused history of the following centuries. The Normans, not content with the lands assigned to them by Henry II, pushed out north and west and south, bringing more and more of Ireland under their control, until it seemed inevitable that they would at last dominate the whole country. Even this threat did not bring the Irish together. Everywhere they resisted the Norman advance; but everywhere their resistance was local and reflected local interests. An Irish king and his people were prepared to fight for their country; but the 'country' they fought for was Breifne or Ossory or Thomond. There was no family, no institution, to symbolize an Ireland in whose cause all could join together. Indeed, local interests were too strong to allow any such feeling to develop: time after time, we find one Irish king allying with the Normans against another in order to pay off old scores or extend his own territory.

Only once, during the whole medieval period, was an attempt made to organize a national campaign; and its history shows clearly how foreign such an idea was to Irish thinking. The attempt did not even originate in

Ireland, but was the product of Scottish policy. Robert Bruce, having secured the independence of Scotland by his victory at Bannockburn, sought to follow up his advantage by attacking English power in Ireland, where he hoped to find allies; and in May 1316 sent over his brother, Edward, with six thousand troops. Edward found some support in the north, which had longstanding connections with Scotland, and he had himself proclaimed 'king of Ireland'; but elsewhere his reception was very different. Though he reached the outskirts of Dublin and penetrated as far westward as Limerick, winning battles and ravaging the country-side as he went, the Irish showed little inclination to respond to the appeal that King Robert had addressed to them on his brother's behalf, urging them to combine with the Scots 'so that with God's help your nation may be able to recover her ancient liberty'. Some joined Edward, as much out of fear as out of enthusiasm for his cause; some resisted him; more took advantage of the general confusion to reoccupy lands they had lost to the Normans, who were now too hard pressed by the invasion to defend them effectively. But there was no general recognition of this 'king of Ireland', no upsurge of national feeling. The Irish could not attempt to follow Scottish example because it sprang from a tradition of national unity of which they had no experience. The concept of a national king, who should exercise real authority over the whole country, impose his will on local rulers and direct the policy of the nation, was probably beyond their comprehension; and it certainly represented a system of government for which they had no desire. The annalists who record the events of these years, and who probably reflect the general opinion, speak of Edward Bruce as a 'usurper'; and they record his final defeat by an Anglo-Norman force with obvious approval: 'Edward Bruce, the destroyer of all Ireland in general, both foreigner and Gael, was slain by the foreigners of Ireland, through the power of battle and bravery . . . and no better deed for the men of all Ireland was wrought from the beginning of the world.'

Irish failure to join with Bruce in a war of national liberation did not indicate satisfaction with things as they were. Local resistance to the Normans continued; and now it took a new turn. Even before the Bruce invasion, the weakness of the colony had begun to appear. The colonial population was too small to defend the territories occupied; many great lords who held Irish lands were absentees and neglected their responsibilities; those who did live in Ireland were apt to quarrel among themselves; English kings, instead of strengthening the colony, weakened it by drawing off men and money for their wars elsewhere. These weaknesses became more and more evident as time went on; and the Irish took full advantage of them. The area under Norman control steadily declined; and in many areas where Norman settlers managed to remain in control they lost any regular contact with royal authority and frequently abandoned their own traditions for a Gaelic way of life. But, just as the Irish had refused to combine against Norman power when it was growing, so they refused to combine when it was in decay. The area over which the English king, as lord of Ireland, could exercise any regular and effective authority shrank by degrees, until it comprised little more than a narrow strip along the east coast—the 'English Pale'—defended with difficulty from the incursions of the Irish who hung along its borders. Yet, even so, his claim to lordship over the whole country was never formally disputed. The resurgent Irish set up no rival government, made no claim to national independence, showed no sign of readiness to combine under a single leader. Local rulers maintained and defended a local independence; but, when it suited their purposes, or when the royal forces seemed, for the time being, dangerously strong, they were always ready to submit to the king's authority, declare that they were his loyal subjects and promise faithful service for the future.

(3)

The coming of the Normans divided the political and social life of Ireland into two; and on both sides of the line the division was soon accepted as a permanent feature of Irish life. To the colonists, it was basically territorial: they distinguished between the colonized area, the lands *inter Anglos*, and the area controlled by the natives, the lands *inter Hibernicos*. The distinction made by the Irish was more emphatically racial: they spoke of the colonists as 'the foreigners of Ireland', people who had an established place in the country, but who yet remained foreign to the Gaels. This division, modified from time to time in externals but retaining its essential character, was to dominate the course of Irish history.

It was natural that the colonists should emphasize the territorial character of the division. The distinguishing mark of the area under their control was not its population, in which the natives remained preponderant, but the way in which it was governed. Wherever the Normans went they brought with them the whole structure of feudal society. They carved out lordships and manors, founded towns, endowed monasteries and reproduced as nearly as they could the pattern of life to which they had been accustomed in England or on the continent. In Ireland, as elsewhere, feudal society rested on a hierarchy of authority; and at the top of this hierarchy stood the king of England, in his capacity as lord of Ireland. Henry II had regarded the lordship as personal to himself and separable from the crown of England: he had transferred it to his son, John, at a time when it was by no means certain that John would ever become king. But with John's accession in 1199 the crown and the lordship were once more united and were ever after regarded as indissolubly linked. Ireland and England were thus parts of the same monarchy, though ruled under different titles; and England was the seat of the monarchy and the main source of its power. This close connection necessarily affected both the character of the lordship and the status of its inhabitants.

Since Ireland was a distinct possession, it must have an administration of its own. Since the colonists, whatever their origins, were regarded as English, they were entitled to English liberties. It followed, therefore, that the government of the lordship should be modelled on that of England. Whether or not things were consciously thought out in these terms, this was the result. At the head of the administration stood a chief governor, representing the king and entitled, according to the terms of his appointment, justiciar, lord lieutenant, or lord deputy; and, like the king in England, he was assisted by a council of ecclesiastics and laymen. The judicial system, though it started from small beginnings in the early days of the colony, came in time to reproduce the English pattern; and the law it administered was the common law of England. The colonized area was cut up into shires and liberties; and the taxes due from them were paid, as in England, into an exchequer. Constitutional developments in England were followed, though not without some delay, in Ireland; and before the end of the thirteenth century parliament had become a regular institution, with a lower house containing representatives of counties, cities and boroughs, and an upper house of spiritual and temporal lords. The desire to keep the two countries parallel is strikingly illustrated by the grant of Magna Carta to Ireland in 1217, two years after it had been granted in England. Later generations in Ireland were to appeal to it with the same enthusiasm and the same lack of historical understanding as their English contemporaries.

In practice, this system of government operated only within the colonized areas; and in the later Middle Ages its effective power hardly reached beyond the narrow limits of the Pale. But, in name and in legal theory, it was a government for the whole country; and it represented the first serious attempt to provide Ireland with an organized central administration. Even at its weakest, it retained a symbolic importance as the only secular institution that claimed, or could claim, authority over the whole population and over every part of the country. The tradition of a Gaelic High Kingship was dead; and the political thinking of the native Irish rulers extended no further than a determination to keep control of their own territories and wage war on those of their neighbours. In these circumstances, the Dublin administration, simply by continuing to exist, established itself as the one fixed point in the Irish political scene, as the only possible nucleus round which a united Ireland might eventually be built up. The very notion of an Irish state with an effective central government is part of Ireland's English heritage.

The government of the lordship, whatever its claims or its significance for the future, was, in practice, a government for the colony; and it was based on a conscious division of the population into colonial and native, English and Irish. The officials who manned its institutions were English, by birth or by descent; its parliaments represented only the colonized areas; the native Irish, unless they had been specifically admitted to the benefits of English law, had no access to its courts. This exclusiveness may be traced to the strength of the English connection. Had Henry II been content to ignore events in Ireland, had he left Strongbow and his companions to themselves, there would probably have emerged a mixed community in which Norman and Gaelic traditions would have been combined. But the king's intervention and his establishment of a central administration under his own control led to the planting of English institutions in Ireland and encouraged further colonization, not only by knights and soldiers, but also by merchants, artisans and husbandmen. The closer the link with England and the larger the English population, the more likely it was that the barrier between colonist and native would be maintained.

From the beginning, the settlers regarded English blood as a badge of superiority and had a typically colonial contempt for the natives. This attitude, originally encouraged by military success against vastly superior numbers, survived even after the Irish had begun to recover much of the ground they had lost. It is true that many of the English in the more sparsely colonized areas succumbed under this Irish advance and took to using the Irish language, Irish dress, Irish hair-styles, even Irish names. But this only confirmed the hard core of the colony in a determination to remain English.

Their determination is clearly expressed in the legislation generally known as the Statutes of Kilkenny, enacted at a parliament held there in 1366. The purpose was to maintain and strengthen the barrier between the two races: alliance between them by marriage, concubinage or fostering of children was prohibited; Englishmen were not to dress or ride in the Irish fashion or take Irish names; neither the English nor the Irish living among the English were to use the Irish language; no Irishman was to be appointed to any ecclesiastical office in the English areas. These measures have often been seen as an aggressive outlawing of the native Irish; they were, in fact, a desperate attempt to check the decay of the colony and to preserve it from being completely submerged. And the attempt was only partly successful. Though the three archbishops and five bishops present at Kilkenny published sentence of excommunication against all who should contravene the statutes, they were frequently broken, even by some of those who had helped to pass them. It proved, in the end, impossible to maintain a rigid line of division between colonist and native.

But the line, however blurred, did not disappear. The ordinary citizens of the Pale, closely linked with England by trade and proud of their English heritage, looked with mingled contempt and fear on the 'wild Irish' and 'degenerate English' whose incessant wars threatened life and property. The nobles and gentry who remained loyal to the crown never forgot that they were English by blood. Political expediency might make them tolerant of the Irish and ready, on occasion, to form Irish alliances; but with many of them a traditional hostility towards the natives was never far below the surface.

A striking example of the survival and force of this hostility may be found in a famous episode of the early sixteenth century. On 19 August 1504 a battle was fought at Knocktoe, a few miles east of Galway. The leader on one side was Ulick Burke of Clanrickard, a typical example of the 'degenerate English'. His opponent was Gerald FitzGerald, eighth earl of Kildare, the most powerful man in Ireland and, as Henry VII's deputy, head of the Dublin administration. But, though both leaders were of Anglo-Norman descent, their armies displayed that intermixture of colonial and native forces that was characteristic of all the major Irish engagements of the period. After a furious contest, FitzGerald won a crushing victory, whereupon Lord Gormanston, a noble of the Pale who had fought beside him in the battle, turned and said: 'We have for the most part killed our enemies, and if we do the like with the Irishmen that are with us, it were a good deed.' To him, the native Irish, on whatever side they might fight, were still the natural enemies of his race.

Kildare's outlook was much less simple and straightforward. He had none of Gormanston's contempt for the natives. He mingled on terms of equal friendship with Irish rulers, he encouraged Gaelic learning and literature. Yet these broad sympathies did not affect the essential character of his position. He remained a great feudal lord, intensely proud of his descent and bound by tradition no less than by office to maintain the rights of the English crown in Ireland. It was to the king that he looked as the source of authority and honour. He managed to persuade Henry that the battle of Knocktoe, which was in fact a conflict between rival factions in Ireland, had been a victory for royal authority, and he was rewarded with the order of the Garter.

Some historians have seen in Kildare and others like him, men who remained loyal to the king but who were at the same time sympathetic to Gaelic culture, the nucleus of a 'middle nation', in which both sections of the population might eventually have come together. But there was no institutional framework within which such a blending of races could take place. The native Irish had never had any share in the government of the lordship; the 'degenerate English' had, as far as they could, cut themselves off from it; and there was no alternative institution through which different sections of the population could be drawn together. Even the church was divided into areas of 'English' and 'Irish' influence; and racial animosity could be quite as strong, and sometimes almost as violent, among the clergy as among the laity. Only in the fluctuating pattern of military alliances, which formed the stuff of Irish politics, could such combinations take place; but these were, by their nature, limited in scope and uncertain in duration. They contributed nothing towards any genuine mingling of different traditions to form a consciously united people. On the one side, the native Irish, as divided as ever among themselves, lacked any sense of common purpose; on the other, the hard core of the colony, which was concentrated in the area around Dublin, remained as firmly as ever attached to its English traditions and proud of its English blood.

This is not to say, however, that the outlook of the colonists underwent no change. Conflict with the natives kept alive their consciousness of being English; but they soon came to regard Ireland as their country and to develop a sense of corporate identity. They were, to use their own language, 'the English of Ireland', 'the English nation of this land'; and, as such, they had rights of their own, with which the 'English of England' could not interfere. Like other colonists, they were suspicious of authority claimed by the mother country; and they were particularly jealous of newly arrived officials who, being English by birth, might look down upon those who were merely 'English by blood'. An attempt in Edward III's reign to ensure that all judicial offices should be filled by lawyers sent over from England aroused the same sort of indignation as Swift was to express four hundred years later at the appointment of English-born bishops to Irish sees.

This parallel between the fourteenth century and the eighteenth is not merely adventitious. It indicates a real continuity of tradition: claims developed during the medieval period were passed on, not merely from one generation to another but from the descendants of the first colonists to those newcomers who, in a later age, ousted them from their estates and took over their positions of influence. The constitutional programme of Anglo-Irish patriots in the reign of George III was consciously derived from precedents set by the 'English of Ireland' three or four hundred years earlier.

(4)

It was in the latter half of the fifteenth century that the Dublin administration attained its greatest measure of independence. England was distracted by the Wars of the Roses; and English kings had little time to spare for the affairs of Ireland. Even the accession of the Tudors made little immediate difference: Kildare, the victor of Knocktoe, who had ruled as deputy under Edward IV and Richard III, remained in office under Henry VII. All government was conducted in the name of the king, as lord of Ireland; but Kildare's own authority was little less than regal. He summoned parliaments, disposed of the revenue, conducted negotiations with native Irish rulers, commanded the forces of the Pale and defended its borders. From the king's point of view, this system of government had the great advantage of being inexpensive, for it required no support, either in men or in money, from England; and when Kildare died, in 1513, his son succeeded him in the deputyship almost as naturally as in the earldom.

By this time, however, the men who guided English policy, and Wolsey in particular, had come to regard the quasi-independence of the Dublin administration as a dangerous anomaly. There was no abrupt change of policy; but Irish affairs were brought under closer supervision and an attempt was made to undermine the dominant influence of the house of Kildare. One can see, in retrospect, that if the old practice of leaving Ireland to look after itself were to be abandoned the only viable alternative would be a military conquest of the whole country; but many decades were to pass before English statesmen could bring themselves to face this costly undertaking; and it was not completed until the very end of the Tudor period. In the interval, the Reformation had changed the whole situation; and the belated imposition of political unity followed, and was vitiated by, the introduction of a new element of discord.

There was another new element in the situation, which was to exercise a strong and continuing influence on royal policy. Now, for the first time, England's continental enemies began to regard Ireland as a possible base for operations against England itself; and they were encouraged in this by Henry VIII's breach with Rome. Within Ireland, Henry's ecclesiastical revolution aroused little immediate opposition: ecclesiastics and laymen, colonists and natives, had alike been willing to renounce the authority of the pope and accept royal supremacy. But this acquiescent attitude changed in face of Henry's efforts to establish a more direct control over the administration; and he found himself reluctantly involved in years of sporadic warfare. Outwardly, he had some success. Foreign attempts at intervention were foiled; all the great men of the country made formal submission; his newly assumed title of 'King of Ireland' was generally recognized. When he died, there was at least the appearance of peace throughout Ireland. But the appearance was deceptive; and the attempt to impose the Protestant Reformation in the reign of Edward VI was almost everywhere resisted. The resumption of this policy by Elizabeth left Ireland open to the intrigues of her most dangerous enemy, Philip of Spain; and it was the Spanish threat that at last forced Elizabeth, much against her will, to embark on a full-scale war of conquest. When she died, the last resistance had been broken and all Ireland lay, for the first time, open to the authority of the English crown.

This long period of fluctuating policy, foreign intervention, ecclesiastical revolution and military conquest had put a heavy strain on the 'English of Ireland' and left them in a dubious position. The power of the great colonial families—the FitzGeralds, the de Burgos and the rest—had been broken. The semi-independence of the colony had gone. Since the 1530s the Dublin administration had been directed by a series of English-born viceroys supported by English troops. What the future might hold was still obscure; and the 'English of Ireland' regarded it with anxious eyes.

One reason for their anxiety lay in the religious position. At the beginning of Elizabeth's reign acts of supremacy and uniformity were pushed through a parliament in Dublin; and, so far as the framework of ecclesiastical organization was concerned, the Irish church had been brought gradually into line with the English. But Elizabeth had been no missionary zealot; and, throughout her reign, those who refused to conform—the 'recusants'—had, in general, been left free to follow their own way in religion, provided they were loyal to the crown in matters of politics. Among the native Irish and 'degenerate English' religion and politics had generally gone together; and their resistance to the crown, fomented and supported by the papacy and by Spain, had taken on the character of a religious war. But the English of the Pale and of the cities and towns throughout the country could not so easily forget their traditional loyalties. Even if the crown had not always been able to rely upon their support, their attitude had certainly eased the work of conquest. But, now that it was completed, could they count on a continuance of a toleration that had been dictated largely by political necessity?

Among the land-owning classes, this anxiety over religion was closely linked with anxiety over their estates. The crown was naturally concerned to strengthen the small Protestant population; and one obvious way of doing this was by a policy of colonization, or, in the language of the time, 'plantation'. Already, in Elizabeth's reign, the process had begun: estates confiscated from rebels had been let out to new settlers. So far, the influx had been small; but it was quite large enough to alarm the older colonists. They knew how easily the titles of their estates might be impugned by crown lawyers; and they saw with dismay how frequently English adventurers, backed by royal favour, were able to acquire lands and influence: now that the conquest had been completed, it seemed likely that the number of those seeking to establish themselves in Ireland would increase.

In 1603, when James VI of Scotland succeeded to the kingdoms of England and Ireland, the old colonists were still loyal to the crown, still ready to maintain their traditional rôle as the 'English of Ireland'. But circumstances had changed; and they were no longer the only, or even the main, basis of royal authority. The foundation of a new colony had been laid, small as yet in numbers, but strong in influence. Already the way was open for a conflict of interests, later to become a conflict of arms, between these 'New English' settlers, who found in Ireland an area for exploitation more convenient and more profitable than America, and the 'Old English', whose ancestors had established England's first colony in the reign of Henry II.

II

The Foundation of
Protestant Ascendancy

(1)

In 1603 the Old English looked anxiously to the future. Yet their anxiety was not unmingled with hope; for they had, after all, established some claim on the gratitude of the government. If many of them had resisted the advance of English power during the Elizabethan wars and had joined the native Irish in insurrection, many more had stood firm to the crown. The loyalty of the towns, in particular, had been of immense importance. During the last decade of Elizabeth's reign, when Hugh O'Neill's rebellion in Ulster and his spectacular victory at the Yellow Ford had set all Ireland ablaze, the towns had remained as islands of English influence. The final victory, which brought all Ireland for the first time effectively under the crown, had been an achievement of the old colonists as well as of the new armies that a frightened English government had poured across the channel. But, though the Old English had contributed to the victory, its very completeness tended to undermine their position. They had a claim, certainly, to the favour of the crown; but it was doubtful if they had the means of enforcing it. In a sense, they had made the worst of both worlds. Their political loyalty had ensured an English victory so crushing that there seemed little hope of successful resistance at a later date. But, at the same time, their refusal to conform to crown policy in religion kept them under constant suspicion of being only half-hearted in their allegiance; and the memory of their past services was overlaid by fears for their future conduct.

In these circumstances, it was the constant aim of the Old English to persuade the government of their continuing loyalty. Though they did not waver in ecclesiastical allegiance to Rome, they tried, on all occasions, to demonstrate that recusancy in religion was perfectly compatible with devotion to the crown in all secular matters. And they were at pains to emphasize not only their loyalty but their 'Englishness': families that had, in the past, become so far merged with the native population as to

28

abandon their English surnames now thought it expedient to resume them, and, with them, English dress and English ways of life.

In spite of the suspicion that their recusancy inevitably drew upon them, the Old English were not without means of defending themselves. Even after the confiscations of Elizabeth's reign they still held about half the land of the kingdom; they dominated its commercial life; they were strongly established in the legal profession. Though the central administration was, for the most part, in the hands of English-born officials and new English settlers, the Old English nobility and gentry supplied much of the framework of local government, and most of the cities and towns were ruled by Old English magistrates. They thus held a strong position within the constitution, and a position of which they could not easily be deprived: however doubtfully Protestant opinion might regard them, Ireland could hardly be governed without their co-operation.

There was another, and even more cogent, reason why the crown could not afford to alienate the Old English. Ireland was but newly reduced to obedience. The spirit of resistance was still alive among the native Irish; and there was good reason to fear that they might easily be stirred to fresh insurrection by the prospect of foreign help. If the Old English were pushed to a similar state of discontent the cost of holding Ireland down would be far beyond the resources of James I or Charles I. For them, the only practicable policy was to treat the Old English with respect, to listen to their grievances, and encourage them to believe that they would obtain redress within the framework of the constitution and in return for loyalty to the crown. Government officials in Ireland, influenced by the aggressive Protestantism that characterized many of the more recent settlers, sometimes ran counter to this cautious policy and attempted to put the laws against recusancy into strict operation. But such action received no encouragement and little support from London; and the Old English found that when they were threatened with persecution an appeal to the king and council usually brought them relief.

During the early decades of the seventeenth century, then, the Old English continued to exercise a good deal of political influence; they enjoyed a large measure of religious toleration; and over much of the country they retained a hold on the local administration. But they had little security for the future. The crown, though obliged by circumstances to temporize with recusancy, would always prefer to rely upon Protestant support; and during this period it endeavoured to build up the small Protestant population of Ireland by reviving the old policy of 'plantation'. This policy had its greatest success in Ulster, where thousands of English and Lowland Scots were settled on lands confiscated from the native Irish; but elsewhere also—in Leitrim, in Wexford, in King's County—new Protestant colonies were established. This was a development full of danger to the Old English. Every Protestant family brought over to Ireland, every acre of Irish soil transferred to Protestant ownership, reduced the relative strength of their position, and brought nearer the time when the crown, no longer obliged to play for their support, could grant or withhold its favours at discretion.

Though the Old English had little sympathy with the native Irish proprietors, at whose expense these plantations were made, they were uneasy at the steady influx of new settlers; and they were aware that the practice of reviving dormant royal claims to land, in which the crown lawyers had shown an unscrupulous ingenuity, was a threat to their own estates also. But they could see no alternative to the settled policy of loyalty which had hitherto helped them to defend their position even if they had been unable to strengthen it. Their loyalty was not, however, merely self-interested. It was part of the tradition they had inherited from the past, a symbol of the English ancestry of which they were still proud. What they aimed at was to secure from the crown, by peaceful negotiation, a guarantee of freedom in the exercise of their religion, security for their estates and a larger share in the administration of the kingdom. These were hopes that they never willingly abandoned. Even when, at the end of 1641, they joined the native Irish of Ulster in rebellion against the royal administration in Dublin, they continued to assert their loyalty to the king and declared that their only object was to defend themselves against the policy pursued by the 'puritan faction' in England, whose triumph would be as disastrous to the monarchy as to themselves. But whatever the motives of the Old English may have been, however great were the pressures under which they acted, the decision they took in 1641 marked, for them, the beginning of the end. It was to lead to confiscation of their estates, destruction of their political influence and, eventually, to their disappearance as a distinct group in the population of Ireland.

(2)

The period 1603–41 can be seen in retrospect as a decisive stage in the decline of the Old English. It was no less decisive in the rise of the New English who were to take their place. Though the line of division that separated the two groups was already clear in religion, it was not yet so sharply marked in politics as it was later to become. There was, it is true, continuous rivalry between them; but both Old and New English acted within the same constitutional framework; both could influence, in some measure, the policy of the crown and its representatives in Ireland; and, despite their mutual hostility, there was an area of common concern in which it paid them, at least from time to time, to co-operate. In the development of the New English it is the co-operation rather than the hostility that gives this period a peculiar importance; in their occasional alliance with their Old English rivals they learned to regard themselves as the inheritors and protectors of Ireland's constitutional rights as a distinct kingdom; and from this it was no great step to the claim implicitly made by their eighteenth-century successors to be, in fact, the Irish nation.

Co-operation between the two groups had its most significant results in parliament. Under Elizabeth, parliaments had almost ceased in Ireland: only three were held during the whole reign. But in the more settled conditions of the early seventeenth century it was natural that they should be revived, and that the crown should look to them not only for legislation but also for financial assistance. James I, in the hope of securing a docile House of Commons, created a great many new boroughs; 'the more the merrier', was his answer to the complaint that he had been over lavish. But though these means ensured that there should be a Protestant majority, the parliament that he summoned was neither easily controlled nor generous in its grants of money. Wentworth, later Earl of Strafford, who governed Ireland for Charles I from 1632 onwards, was much more successful; and the parliaments of this period granted the large subsidies that were asked of them.

These parliaments saw some fierce disputes between Old and New English, for the former naturally resented the numerical inferiority to which they had been reduced in the Commons, an inferiority sharply at variance with their superior strength in the country as a whole, and especially in the ancient cities and boroughs. Nevertheless, the two sides had a common interest in resisting demands for money. Wentworth, so long as his power seemed unassailable, was able to beat down all opposition and, when it suited him, to play off Old and New English against each other. But both parties hated as well as feared him: the Old English because his scheme for a vast new plantation in Connaught threatened them with a progressive confiscation of their estates; the New English because he deliberately excluded them from any real influence in the administration. Old English and New English alike were alienated by his policy of 'thorough', which involved a ruthless enforcement of all the rights claimed by the crown, backed up by the extraordinary jurisdiction of the court of Castle Chamber (the Irish version of Star Chamber) and of the council, which was dominated by dependants of the viceroy and did little more than register his decisions. Once Wentworth's authority was threatened at its source, in England, it was bound to be attacked in Ireland also.

This was, in fact, the situation in the summer of 1640. Royal authority was being openly defied in Scotland; the Short Parliament, called at Wentworth's suggestion, had shown the strength of English opposition to the crown; Wentworth himself was with the king, and was still his principal adviser, but his policy was crumbling around him. In these circumstances, the Irish parliament, until recently his docile instrument, turned sharply against him; and a hostile majority, made up of Old English recusants and New English Protestants, took control of the House of Commons. To begin with, their main concern was to denounce the government of Wentworth as tyrannical. But denunciation of wrongs led by natural progress to assertion of rights; and soon their main theme was the claim of Ireland to be governed according to the terms of her own constitution. The New English supported this claim as readily as they had supported the initial attack on Wentworth and joined their Old English allies in demanding redress of national grievances.

Something of the basis and character of this alliance will appear from a consideration of the views put forward by two of its leading members, Patrick Darcy and Audley Mervyn. Darcy was an Old English recusant from County Galway, and was probably the ablest constitutional lawyer in the House; it was to him that the Commons entrusted the detailed defence of the 'Queries' they had drawn up as a statement of their views on a wide range of constitutional issues. Mervyn, in contrast, was a native of Hampshire and a newcomer to Ireland, who had received lands in the Ulster plantation and, later on, a military appointment in the province. Like many of the New English, he tended to favour a puritan outlook in religion; and this may have helped to account for his opposition to Wentworth, whose ecclesiastical policy in Ireland had been guided by Archbishop Laud. It was he who opened the case against four members of the Wentworth administration impeached by the House of Commons in March 1641.

Despite wide differences in background and outlook Darcy and Mervyn were at one in expounding and defending the constitutional rights of Ireland. Though there is some difference of emphasis, it does not fall exactly where one might have expected. Darcy insists on the identity of the Irish constitution with the English: 'if any man ask the question by what law we are governed, there is no proper answer other than by the law of England'; and it is on this basis that he defends the sole right of the Irish parliament to legislate for Ireland. He goes out of his way to profess an unbounded loyalty to the crown:

> Before the least flower in his majesty's royal garland should wither, we shall be ready to water the same with showers of our blood, even to the last drop, in his majesty's service, and with our lives and substance will maintain the just prerogative of our gracious lord King Charles and his posterity, whom we pray God to flourish on earth over us and ours, until all flesh be convoked before the last great tribunal.

For Darcy, the rights of prince and subject were interdependent; and he found the basis both of authority and of liberty in the common law and Magna Carta.

Mervyn had none of Darcy's erudition; and his speech at the opening of the impeachment proceedings was couched in the tediously artificial style for which he later made himself notorious. Yet it is in its own way a remarkable performance. The treason that he alleges against the accused is not treason against the crown, but against the law and constitution of Ireland; and Mervyn, an Englishman born and bred, presents the case of his adopted country under a figure that has an established place in the long tradition of Irish patriotism:

> This kingdom, personated in the sable habit of a widow, with dishevelled hairs, seems to petition your lordships, that since she is a mother to most of us, yet certainly a nurse unto us all, you would make some order for redress of her tyrannical oppression.

Mervyn may not have been, at heart, very much concerned about the grievances of the Old English; but since he and his fellow-settlers had committed themselves to a life in Ireland he was determined that they should enjoy the liberties to which they felt they were entitled; and these were the liberties that he claimed in the name of the Irish constitution.

The alliance between Old and New English was broken by the Ulster insurrection of October 1641; and the long discussion over points of law gave way to more bloody argument. But there had been time for the New English to learn that Ireland had, or ought to have, a constitution, that in Ireland as in England it was possible to appeal to the common law and Magna Carta. A time was to come, in the not very distant future, when they would look on these rights as their own exclusive possession and forget, or ignore, the claims of the great mass of their fellow-countrymen. But when that time came the New English had ceased to regard themselves as 'new'; and, though they never ceased to assert their claim to the liberties of Englishmen, they were already half convinced that they constituted the 'Irish nation'.

(3)

The insurrection of 1641 brought in two decades of civil war and social upheaval that left a permanent mark on Irish life and on the character of Ireland's relations with England. Even before 1641 Irish affairs had become inextricably mixed up with the political crisis that was reaching its climax in Great Britain; and the parliamentary victory in England was followed, perhaps inevitably, by a new conquest of Ireland, a conquest with which the name of Cromwell is for ever associated in the memory of Irishmen. And conquest was followed, no less inevitably, by confiscation. Throughout the country almost every Roman Catholic proprietor was forced to surrender at least part of his property and many lost everything. Protestant royalists who had failed to come to terms with the new régime suffered a similar fate. In this way millions of acres of land and a vast quantity of urban property passed into the control of the state. Ireland thus lay open for a new plantation, greater than any that had yet taken place. The confiscated lands and houses were allocated to Englishmen who had advanced money to finance the war, to soldiers whose pay was in arrears, to army contractors whose bills were still unpaid, to influential officials, civil and military, of the Commonwealth government. Both in town and country a large new propertied class was established, Protestant in religion and mainly, though not exclusively, English by birth.

These new colonists, numerous and powerful as they were, had no monopoly of property or influence. A substantial section of the Protestant population established before 1641 had survived the period of war and conquest. If they had supported the king at one stage of the struggle they had changed sides in time to save their estates; and many of them managed to secure additional grants of land under the Commonwealth. Thus there was, among the Protestant ruling class of the 1650s, a strong leavening of men whose political outlook had been formed in the Ireland of pre-war days and who could link the newcomers with a tradition of which they would otherwise have been ignorant. But the whole class was bound together by a firm determination to hold on to the estates they had won:

loyalty to their property was a loyalty from which they would never swerve. When the turn of events made it expedient to call King Charles home again and restore the monarchy, they were forward in promoting the change and loud in their declarations of devotion to the crown. The result did not entirely answer their expectations; for Charles showed himself inconveniently concerned about the welfare of his Roman Catholic subjects, and within a few years of the Restoration those who had received grants from the Commonwealth government had been obliged to surrender a proportion of their estates. But the final effect of the Cromwellian settlement, even after it had been modified in this way, was to transform the distribution of property in Ireland. About four-fifths of the whole country was now in the hands of Protestant proprietors; and the cities and towns, even those that had formerly been strongholds of Old English influence, were wholly under Protestant control.

This transformation meant much more than a change in the balance of property and influence. It gave a new intensity and a new meaning to the cleavage between Roman Catholic and Protestant; from this time onward religion and politics were more closely identified than ever before. It was a development of fatal consequence for the Old English, whose position had depended on keeping the two apart. They could survive as a distinct group only so long as the government was willing to accept their English ancestry and traditional loyalty to the crown as a counterweight to their non-conformity in religion. But their junction with the Ulster insurgents in 1641 and their subsequent conduct had seemed to confirm the common Protestant suspicion that papists, whether Irish or English, could never be relied upon. It is true that the Old English had not only asserted their own loyalty but had also received from their native Irish allies a declaration that they too were acting as loyal subjects of the king. In fact, however, what held the two groups together was not a common devotion to King Charles, in whose name they professed to act, but a common religious faith; and the influence of religion appears in all their actions. The system of government that they set up at Kilkenny was formed under the direction of their bishops. In all their formal documents they described themselves as 'The Confederate Catholics of Ireland'. Like the Scottish covenanters, by whose example they were influenced, they supported their authority by a religious sanction: the 'oath of association', which they enforced wherever their power extended, was to be taken by all under pain of excommunication. The first item of their declared programme was to secure the rights of the church; and, though they included also the prerogatives of the crown and the liberties of the nation, the main stumbling block in all negotiations for peace was the claim they put forward on behalf of the Roman Catholic church. If, later on, the victorious Protestants were to conceive of the Irish nation, in a political sense, as exclusively Protestant, the Confederates conceived of it as exclusively Roman Catholic. Between these two concepts there was little possibility of compromise; and the Old English were the first victims of the political rigidity they had helped to create. When the Confederates had been broken, and the last remnants of their military strength destroyed by the Cromwellian forces, the Old English suffered, along with the natives, under the common condemnation passed upon all 'Irish papists'.

After the Restoration, royal intervention enabled many of the Old English nobility and gentry to recover at least part of their estates; but the position of the Old English, as a body, was very different from what it had been before 1641. Neither James I nor Charles I could have afforded to alienate them by a policy of religious persecution; the substantial toleration that they enjoyed in the Restoration period depended simply on royal favour. The basis of their former strength and influence had been hopelessly undermined. Parliament was now a purely Protestant body. Though Roman Catholics might live and trade in the cities and towns, they could not be members of corporations or hold any municipal office. They were excluded from the army and militia, and from all appointments under the crown. They had been, so to speak, pushed outside the constitution; and there was little, now, to distinguish their position from that of the native Irish. From the mid-century onwards Protestant writers commonly lump the two groups together and not infrequently use 'Irishmen' and 'papists' as interchangeable terms. There seemed to be nothing that the Old English could do for themselves. Their fortunes depended wholly on the crown: only Charles's goodwill protected them from more oppressive measures; and their one chance of recovery lay, as the reign of James II was to show, in a radical change of royal policy.

The circumstances that depressed the position of the Old English enhanced that of the Protestants. Greatly strengthened in numbers and wealth, encouraged by military victory, holding a monopoly of political influence, they were more confident than ever before of their power to defend themselves and to stand on their own feet. This confidence no doubt underlay their readiness to assert the constitutional rights of Ireland. Early in 1660, while the negotiations that led to the Restoration were still in progress, a Protestant convention in Dublin repudiated the Cromwellian system of a central legislature for the whole British Isles and declared that Ireland had a right to be governed by parliaments of her own, basing their claim on 'the laws and laudable custom and constitution of this nation', as established for many hundreds of years. This is a declaration entirely in line with the arguments put forward by the House of Commons before the insurrection; and it is not surprising to find Audley Mervyn, the champion of the Irish constitution in 1641, taking a leading place in the convention. But though the Protestants had learnt their lesson well, they had no mind now to share power with those from whom they had learnt it, the Old English recusants. They demanded, and secured, a parliament of Protestant lords and commons; and they used it, as far as they could, to curtail the royal favour towards those who had been dispossessed under the Commonwealth. In their view, the Ireland whose rights they were so ready to assert was to be a Protestant kingdom.

(4)

It would be misleading to represent the seventeenth-century wars, out of which the Irish Protestants emerged as an exclusive ruling class, simply as wars of religion. The contest was one between a long-established population, native Irish or Old English in origin, on the one hand, and a growing body of new colonists on the other. But it was inevitable that religion should soon be accepted as the dividing line, for it was the most obvious mark of distinction between the two groups: the newcomers were almost exclusively Protestant, while their opponents were Roman Catholic. The force of this distinction was so great that it tended to overshadow every other consideration; and the side a man took in the conflict depended less on his origin than on his religious allegiance. Lord Castlehaven, for example, was the grandson of an Ulster planter of James I's reign, and may be reckoned among the newest of the New English, for he made his first visit to Ireland in 1641; but, because he was a Roman Catholic, he eventually joined the Confederates and fought along with the Old English and native Irish armies. The same tendency could work in the opposite direction also. Murrough O'Brien, Lord Inchiquin, represented a union of Gaelic monarchy and Old English aristocracy: he was descended, on his father's side, from the ancient royal house of Munster; his mother, Ellen FitzGerald, belonged to 'the blood of the first conquest', and traced her ancestry to Gerald of Windsor, the most famous of Strongbow's companions. But Inchiquin was a Protestant; and throughout the 1640s he maintained the Protestant cause in Munster, sometimes on behalf of the king, sometimes on behalf of parliament, but always with a ruthless courage which neither shrank from a powerful enemy nor spared a weak one. There was no Englishman in Ireland whom the Confederate Catholics hated and feared so much as this terrible descendant of Brian Boru. This religious distinction, the decisive influence of which is so strikingly illustrated in the careers of Castlehaven and Inchiquin, received new and lasting force at the Restoration, when the constitutional settlement gave the Protestants, for the first time, a legal monopoly of political power.

The ascendancy thus established was not finally assured until after the victory of the Williamite forces in the Revolutionary war; but the Revolution made little difference to the character and composition of the community by which this ascendancy was exercised. Most of the families which were to dominate Irish politics in the eighteenth century—indeed, most of the families which made up the rank and file of the Protestant population—were already established in Ireland by the 1660s. During the next hundred years the Anglo-Irish were to acquire greater cohesion and a stronger sense of political purpose; but in the Restoration era they are already emerging as a recognizable group.

The essential characteristic of this group was its Protestantism. The core of the group was made up of New English of the early seventeenth century, their descendants and successors, supplemented by later colonists, mainly of the Cromwellian period; and these were, for the most part, English by birth or by recent descent. But though the English character of the group was so strongly marked that the terms 'English' and 'Protestant' were often used interchangeably, the Protestant population did, in fact, contain a significant number of Old English and native Irish. This number was to be considerably increased in the eighteenth century, when the repressive legislation under which the Roman Catholics suffered induced many of them to conform either in order to save their estates or in hope of professional advancement; but the Old English and native Irish elements were already present before the Revolution.

We can get some indication of the layers of population among the emerging Anglo-Irish ascendancy from a glance at the House of Commons that met in Dublin in May 1661. It contained, as might be expected, a large number of newcomers who had settled in the country during the Commonwealth period. Two may be taken as typical of the rest. John Bligh, member for Athboy, was a London merchant and a member of the Salters' Company, who came to Ireland, after the fighting was over, to manage the affairs of those who had advanced money for the war and were now entitled to be repaid in confiscated Irish lands. Whatever he may have done for his clients, he did very well for himself, acquiring a substantial estate in County Meath. His family continued the good work of looking after their own interests; and his grandson, another John, was raised to the peerage in 1721. John Ponsonby, one of the members for County Kilkenny, was an English country gentleman who had raised troops for the parliamentary cause and had accompanied Cromwell to Ireland in 1649 as a major of horse. Partly by grant from the state, partly by wise speculation, he acquired extensive lands; he strengthened his position by marrying into the peerage; and he founded a family that was to play a leading part in the Irish parliament and, after the union, to provide a Whig leader at Westminster.

Although Cromwellian settlers, whether civilians like Bligh or soldiers like Ponsonby, were numerous in the House, they were not predominant. Many New English families of the earlier seventeenth century had grown in wealth and influence under the Commonwealth, and they formed a powerful group in parliament. Audley Mervyn, for example, was still very much to the fore: against the influence of the court, which favoured another candidate, he secured his own election as Speaker. Typical of this group were the Beresfords—like the Ponsonbys, a family with a great political future. In the parliament in 1661 they were represented by two members, the son and the grandson of an Ulster planter of James I's time. But there were a good many members who, though their families may be classed as New English, could trace an Irish connection back to the sixteenth century. There were three members of the influential Boyle clan, descendants of Richard Boyle, first earl of Cork, an unscrupulous land-grabber of Elizabeth's reign, who had built up vast estates in Munster. With them may be grouped their cousin, Richard Jones, later to become notorious as earl of Ranelagh, the grandson of an Elizabethan cleric who had pushed his way up from obscurity to the archbishopric of Dublin. Other members with this kind of background include Foliot Wingfield and John Edgeworth. The Wingfields, a typical Elizabethan military family, had been established in Ireland for the greater part of a century, and had intermarried both with Old English and with native Irish. The Edgeworths had been settled in County Longford since the 1590s. Their achievement was to lie in literature rather than in politics: the life of the Anglo-Irish gentry in the heyday of their power is nowhere more shrewdly portrayed than in the novels of Maria Edgeworth, great-great-granddaughter of the member for St. Johnstown, County Longford, in the reign of Charles II.

Cromwellians and New English between them made up the great

majority of the House; but the Old English were not wholly unrepresented. Richard Power, the son of an Old English nobleman, had turned Protestant in the 1650s and was elected knight of the shire for Waterford, where his family had long exercised great influence. Sir John FitzGerald, who sat for the borough of Dungarvan, belonged to the Munster branch of the wide-ranging FitzGerald connection. He was a descendant of the seventh earl of Desmond and related to most of the leading families, Gaelic as well as Old English, of the south of Ireland. His father, who was a Protestant, died while John was still a child; and the guardian to whom he was entrusted by the government made sure of his continued conformity by sending him to school at Eton. Carey Dillon came of a family that had been settled in Ireland since the time of Henry II, though it claimed, on the basis of a legend more romantic than credible, to have a much earlier association with the country. His brother, the third earl of Roscommon, had been, according to Anthony à Wood, 'reclaimed from the superstitions of the Romish church' by the efforts of Archbishop Ussher; and either at the same time or later Carey too had become a Protestant. He served under Ormond in the wars of the 1640s; and in 1661 he was returned to parliament for the borough of Banagher. These three are typical of the small Old English group in the house; wherever the Old English turned Protestant their traditional influence could still open the way to political power. But the number of those who had made the change by 1661 was not large; and the Old English members probably did not exceed a score all told. The native Irish had never, at any point, had much share in parliament. But for them, as for the Old English, religion was now the decisive factor, and two of the most famous of the ancient Gaelic dynasties produced Protestant members who sat in this parliament. Henry O'Brien represented County Clare, the old stronghold of his family; and Daniel O'Neill, a cousin of Owen Roe O'Neill, commander of the Confederate forces in Ulster during the 1640s, represented the borough of Downpatrick.

This parliament, in which the composition and character of the Anglo-Irish were first clearly outlined, met under the viceroyalty of a nobleman who was himself a link between the emerging Anglo-Irish and the older tradition of the medieval colony. James Butler, twelfth earl and first duke of Ormond, was the head of a family that had been settled in Ireland since the reign of King John and had risen to great power and influence. His father's early death had made him a ward of the crown, and he was brought up in the Protestant faith, to which he adhered firmly for the rest of his life. Religious conviction and devotion to the monarchy were the guiding principles of his career. During the troubled decade of the 1640s, when almost all his relations joined with the Confederate Catholics, he stood at the head of the royal administration in Dublin; and through the whole of his long negotiations with the Confederates he insisted tenaciously on maintaining the rights of the established church. When, in 1647, he could hold out no longer, it was to the parliamentary forces rather than to the Confederates that he chose to surrender Dublin—if the capital must pass into the hands of rebels it would, he felt, be safer with Protestant rebels than with papists.

At the Restoration Ormond recovered his estates and his influence; and for more than half the period between Restoration and Revolution he governed Ireland as lord lieutenant. Religion and loyalty determined his policy. He was no persecutor, and even at the height of the Popish Plot he resisted all demands for repressive measures against the Roman Catholics; but he was determined to maintain the Protestant constitution of the kingdom. He laboured hard to promote trade and industry; and he opposed, as well as he could, attempts by the English parliament to restrict Irish economic development. But he always considered Ireland in relation to the crown, which was for him the source and centre of all authority. The welfare of the monarchy was the great end at which he aimed; his loyalty was not national but personal, and he could not conceive of a duty to his country that would override his duty to his king.

In his view of the constitution Ormond was old-fashioned, even in his own day. But in his Protestantism he belonged to the future. It is this that gives him his place as a prototype of the Anglo-Irish; and they soon acquired, in an Ireland where Protestantism and power went together, the aristocratic assurance and habit of command that marked all Ormond's actions. But in the reign of Charles II their position was not yet secure. They already regarded Ireland as their own country, almost, one might say, as their own property. But they felt, not without reason, that their ascendancy might still be put in jeopardy; and this awareness of danger weakened their natural self-confidence. Not until after the Revolution could they enjoy the full sense of superiority that arose from the possession of a settled power, unthreatened by anything more serious than sporadic unrest among a leaderless peasantry.

The Restoration period thus marks an intermediate stage in the development of Protestant ascendancy. The Protestants had gained a monopoly of political power, in local as well as in central administration; but the Old English recusants had not yet abandoned hope of recovering what they had lost, and they based their claims on loyalty to the crown and the English connection. If men's minds had not been dominated by the fears and hatreds of the previous twenty years, by bitter memories of insurrection and massacre, of confiscation and banishment, it might still have been possible to draw together the two strands of the English tradition in Ireland, and bring both Old and New English within a common constitutional framework. But the temper of the times was unfavourable to any scheme of comprehension; and religion was to remain the major test of political allegiance in Ireland.

(5)

The dominant position that the Protestants had won under the Commonwealth and had retained at the Restoration was held by a precarious tenure; and for a brief but crowded period the policy of James II threatened to destroy it altogether. With the crown now openly on their side, the Old English recusants were in the ascendant. Their leading political figure, Richard Talbot, earl of Tyrconnell, became the king's deputy in Ireland; and under his direction the whole administration, central and local, civil and military, was remodelled. Some attempt was made to distinguish between religious and political attitudes. Tyrconnell tried to reassure the Protestants by promising protection in return for loyalty; and James, with his eye on English opinion, was particularly anxious to avoid any appearance of persecution. But in the struggle that followed, though a few Protestants felt obliged by conscience to recognize James II as their lawful king, religion formed the essential line of division: the Roman Catholics, whether Old English or native Irish, stood on one side, and the Protestants stood on the other. For a time, the Protestants seemed threatened with total submergence, and only in the north were they able to resist effectively. But the tide was turned back before the walls of Derry; William III came to their rescue; and his victory at the Boyne opened their way to an even more complete domination of the country than they had formerly enjoyed. When the Roman Catholic commanders finally surrendered at Limerick in 1691 they believed that they had secured, by treaty, some protection for their co-religionists; but the Irish parliament refused to abide by the terms the king had accepted: Old English and native Irish were once more involved in a common ruin; and the long period of oppression that followed all but eradicated the memory of any division between them. Among the few families of the nobility and gentry who managed to hold on to their estates some vestige of an Old

English tradition survived; but the Old English as a body were soon merged in the mass of the population.

For the Irish Protestants the Revolutionary war marked the end of a long struggle. Ireland was now theirs, more securely than ever before. The flower of the Jacobite army had passed into the service of France. Such of the Roman Catholic gentry as survived the Williamite confiscation were too weak, and too nervous about their estates, to meddle in politics. There was no leadership, no spirit, no means, to oppose the ascendancy that Protestant Ireland had now, after a century of conflict, established. During that century the outlook of the Protestants had changed with their position. They were no longer, as they had been in the reign of James I, a small group made up mainly of soldiers, government officials and a few recently planted settlers, uncomfortably conscious of being strangers in an unfriendly land. Now they formed a large and well-established population spread through all ranks of society; still a minority, it is true, but a minority whose political and economic strength gave it a dominant position in the country. They had ceased to be the 'New English' and were already beginning to think of themselves as the 'Irish nation'.

III

'The Rise and Fall of the Irish Nation'

(1)

In the hundred years that followed the Revolution the influence and achievement of the Anglo-Irish reached their height. This was their 'great century'—the century of Swift and Berkeley and Burke, of Goldsmith and Sheridan, of Flood and Grattan; the century also of Wolfe Tone and Robert Emmet, who were themselves products of the Protestant ascendancy that they sought to overthrow. It is this century that has stamped its character on Dublin, that has given the provincial cities and towns most of their best buildings and has dotted the countryside with graceful houses, large and small. Irishmen of later generations, however resentful of the political limitations, social injustice and religious intolerance of the eighteenth century, have never been able to free themselves wholly from its influence. Even in the Irish republic of today the ghost of the Protestant ascendancy walks still.

The resentment that the memory of this ascendancy can arouse in Ireland, even now, does not spring simply from the fact that it was a narrow and selfish ruling class. In this respect it did not differ essentially from other eighteenth-century ruling classes, whose defects have become matter for historical analysis rather than for popular execration. What made the Irish situation a source of such long-enduring bitterness was the existence of a religious barrier between rulers and ruled, a barrier so deepened and intensified by the wars of the preceding century that it superseded all others. This is not to say, of course, that no other barriers, social or economic, existed; still less that all Protestants were well-to-do and all Roman Catholics poor. But even the poorest Protestants commonly felt a greater degree of solidarity with the upper ranks of the Protestant community than with Roman Catholics of their own class. Nor was this attitude simply the product of sectarian bigotry: there was a regular gradation in Protestant society, from top to bottom, so that a poor Protestant might, by industry, ability or luck, make his way up not only to

44

wealth but to political power. But the position of the Roman Catholic was entirely different. Though he might (as, indeed, many did) acquire wealth by trade, he was absolutely shut out, simply by his religious profession, from any post of political power. 'Protestant ascendancy' could, and often did, signify something wider than the dominance of the Protestant landed class: it was the supremacy of the Protestants, as a body, over the Roman Catholic majority. In the closing years of the eighteenth century some of the fiercest defenders of this supremacy were to be found among the Protestant peasantry of Ulster; and their descendants were to carry the struggle into a much later period.

Though the distinction that separated the majority and the minority in Ireland must be stated in religious terms, and though there can be no doubt that religious convictions were sincerely held on both sides, we shall misunderstand the situation completely unless we remember that for Irishmen religion was more than the expression of theological belief. Protestant and Roman Catholic were separated by a gulf deeper than that between the Thirty-nine Articles and the Creed of Pope Pius IV. They formed, in fact, two communities, to some extent intermingled and interdependent, but consciously different; and between them lay the memory of conquest and confiscation, massacre and pillage, conspiracy and persecution. In this long struggle religion had determined the side on which a man stood; but the struggle had been one for land and power, and religion had been a badge of difference rather than the main issue in dispute. Though the Williamite wars had left the Protestants supreme and had brought in a long period of peace, there was no real conciliation. Neither side could forget how much had been lost and won. The victors were ever on their guard; the vanquished kept alive their resentment; and the line of division was hardly less sharply marked in peace than it had been in war.

This division, though most commonly expressed in terms of religion, was sometimes spoken of as one of nationality. Writers on both sides, especially during the two or three decades that followed the Revolution, not infrequently used 'Roman Catholic' and 'Irish', 'Protestant' and 'English' as interchangeable terms. The equivalence has some foundation: the Roman Catholics represented a blending of Gaelic and Old English strains; the bulk of the Protestant population was descended from seventeenth-century settlers, English for the most part, but with a large infusion of lowland Scots, especially in the province of Ulster. Exceptions on either side of the line, though certainly not insignificant, were hardly numerous enough to affect the general character of the situation. But descent is less important than environment; and the Protestant settlers of the seventeenth century, like their medieval predecessors, soon identified their own interests with those of their adopted country. Within a generation they were to be found defending the constitutional rights of the kingdom of Ireland; and when the power of their Roman Catholic rivals had been destroyed in the wars of the Revolution they quickly claimed those rights as their own exclusive property. They might still, in some contexts, speak of themselves as 'English' and of the Roman Catholics as 'Irish'—Swift, for example, insists on the difference between 'the savage old Irish' (meaning the Roman Catholics) and 'the English gentry of this kingdom'; but so far as the constitution was concerned 'the Irish people' meant the Protestants.

This was not, of course, a claim that the Roman Catholics could accept; but during the greater part of the eighteenth century they were in no position to put forward, or even indeed to formulate, a counter-claim on their own behalf. Their surviving leaders, as they gradually recovered from the shock of the Revolution settlement, sought little more than some relaxation of the repressive penal code under which they suffered. Gradually, and even before the code had been modified by statute, their position became somewhat easier. Though public employment and the legal profession were closed to them, trade was open; and by the middle of the century there was a growing class of prosperous Roman Catholic merchants. But neither they nor the remaining Roman Catholic landlords wished to incur the displeasure of government by political agitation; they showed that they were ready to identify themselves with the existing régime, and seemed resolved to earn an improvement in their position by good conduct rather than to win it by threats.

It is much more difficult to assess the attitude of the peasantry. Among them, the sense of distinctiveness was much stronger than among their co-religionists of the middle and upper classes; and this was especially so in the extensive Gaelic-speaking areas. But this sense of distinctiveness had little political content. Though vague hopes of a Stuart restoration lingered long and were blended with even vaguer traditions of Gaelic independence, active loyalties were local rather than national. When discontent erupted in violence, as it often did, this also was local; and the enemy was not the state but the landlord or the tithe-proctor. Only in the last decade of the century did the grievances and aspirations of the peasantry merge in an attempt to overthrow the existing régime, and when this happened the two traditions of Irish nationality stood face to face. It was, ironically, under the leadership of Irish Protestants, stimulated by the French Revolution, that the Roman Catholic masses took the first step towards asserting that they, rather than the Protestants, were the true 'people of Ireland'.

This development was to influence profoundly the position and outlook of the Anglo-Irish. But it was hardly even foreshadowed until the 1790s; and during the previous hundred years, while the Protestant ascendancy seemed to be firmly established, the Anglo-Irish could safely regard themselves as 'the Irish nation', the heirs and guardians of the ancient constitution of the kingdom. In their view, the fears and suspicions that divided them from the Roman Catholic majority did not arise from a difference of nationality, or represent a continuing struggle between 'Ireland' and 'England': they were the product of internal rivalry for property and power. Protestants and Catholics alike were citizens of the same kingdom; but the public safety required that the Catholics should be kept in subordination: they had shown themselves unworthy of trust and must be confined to a purely passive rôle in political affairs. The Anglo-Irish, confident of their ability to defend what they held against any challenge at home, were prepared also to defend their constitution against encroachments from across the Channel.

(2)

The 'great century' of the Anglo-Irish spans the period between 1690 and 1800; it begins on the morrow of the Glorious Revolution and ends with the parliamentary union between Ireland and Great Britain. It opens with a mood of confident expectation and closes in bloodshed, disillusionment and a sense of betrayal. The political history of the intervening period is marked by few great events; and the only continuing theme is one of conflict over the constitutional relations between Ireland and England. Both ministry and parliament in London were determined that Ireland should be kept in a subordinate position, subject not only to the executive authority of the British cabinet but also to the legislative authority of the British parliament. The resentment that this policy roused in Ireland varied in intensity from time to time; but it never died away completely, and it could, on occasion, create excitement and agitation both in the House of Commons and in the country. It was only when this resentment had been effectively organized that the Anglo-Irish were at last able to establish the short-lived and half-illusory independence that marked the height of their political achievement.

Even for this imperfect success they had to wait a long time. Yet they had been prompt to assert their constitutional rights, almost before the dust of the Revolutionary warfare had well settled. It seems, at first sight, a surprising move. They had just been rescued from overwhelming disaster. Protestant clergymen who had suffered imprisonment, Protestant landlords who had lost their estates, Protestant officials driven from their posts—all owed the recovery of liberty, lands and influence to English arms. The many thousand Protestants, of all classes, who had found refuge in Britain had been able to return to their homes on the heels of the victorious Williamite forces. More clearly than ever, it might seem, must they recognize that they were the mere protégés of England, nakedly dependent upon English power for their very existence as a community. Prudence, at least, if not gratitude, seemed to require a ready submission to the will of their deliverers. But the Anglo-Irish saw things differently. Their picture of the situation was a simple one: the Roman Catholics had rebelled against the lawful king and had perverted the machinery of government to their own wicked ends; only after a long and costly war, in which the Irish Protestants had played a gallant part, had rebellion been crushed and lawful authority restored. But these events had not in any way affected the constitution of the kingdom; and the Protestants, as loyal subjects, were entitled to enjoy all its benefits. When parliament met in Dublin, in the autumn of 1692, the ministry was taken aback to find that the House of Commons was ready to assert its rights, and the constitutional claims of Ireland, with a vigour and determination that recalled the troubled sessions of 1640-1.

The struggle thus abruptly begun was not kept up for long. The Commons lacked the continuity of tradition and experience needed for a sustained campaign; William pleased them by abandoning his liberal policy towards the Roman Catholics; and when they found that they were not called upon to confirm the Treaty of Limerick in its entirety, they soon became more amenable to government direction. The claims that had so surprised and alarmed the English ministers in 1692 were not, indeed, disowned or forgotten, and they continued to be debated outside parliament; but in parliament itself they were allowed to fall into the background. It is, however, at this period that the constitutional doctrines of the Anglo-Irish found their classic expression in a pamphlet by William Molyneux, one of the members for Dublin University. He was a man of wide learning, the friend and correspondent of Locke, Halley, Flamsteed and other English and continental scholars; and he won a considerable reputation by his work on optics. It was probably under the influence of Locke that he turned his attention to constitutional questions; and the readiness of the English parliament to interfere in Irish affairs led him to reflect on the nature of the relations between the two kingdoms. The line of argument he followed is made clear in the title of his pamphlet: *The Case of Ireland's Being Bound by Acts of Parliament in England, Stated.* Briefly, it comes to this, that Ireland was subject to the crown of England, but not to the English parliament. The two countries were, in fact, sister kingdoms, linked only by a common allegiance, and Ireland had a right to all the constitutional liberties enjoyed by England.

The niceties of constitutional law and precedent, on which Molyneux laid great stress, were understood by few; but the idea that Ireland was a distinct kingdom, with rights of its own, was easily grasped and sure to have a popular appeal. It was this idea that Swift laid hold of and expressed, more vividly and vigorously than Molyneux had been able to do, in the fourth of his *Drapier's Letters.* The English parliament, he asserted, had no more right to make laws for Ireland than the Irish parliament had to make laws for England; and he assured his readers that 'by the laws of God, of nature, of nations, and of your own country, you are and ought to be as free a people as your brethren in England'. 'Am I a free man in England,' he asks elsewhere, 'and do I become a slave in six hours, by crossing the Channel?' It was in support of this claim to constitutional equality that a nationwide movement for legislative independence was later to develop.

The long delay before such a movement became strong enough to gain even an incomplete success was due in part to the character of parliament and in part to the absence of any machinery for organizing public opinion. The Irish electoral system reproduced and exaggerated all the defects of the electoral system of eighteenth-century England; and the House of Commons was a very imperfect representation even of the Protestant population. It was, generally speaking, an easy matter for the executive (nominated and controlled by the ministry in London) to secure and maintain a safe majority. Though there were always a few members— commonly spoken of as the 'Patriots'—ready to stand up for the rights of Ireland against the claims of England, and though they might, on rare occasions and on special issues, win the temporary support of the House, there seemed for a long time no possibility that the Commons, as a body, would ever commit themselves wholeheartedly to the doctrines of Molyneux and Swift. They were not entirely insensitive to public opinion; but public opinion itself was vague and unorganized. It could be roused now and then on particular questions; speeches would be made and resolutions passed; and country gentlemen would drink patriotic toasts. But there was nothing to keep excitement alive or to give it effective direction; and soon all would sink back into discontented apathy.

What changed the situation was the American colonists' assertion of their rights and their revolt against British authority. The Anglo-Irish saw a parallel to their own situation; and public opinion became excited and expectant. But all this would have produced little positive result had not the entry of France into the war in 1778 brought with it the possibility of invasion. So many of the troops normally stationed in Ireland had been sent abroad that the government had to confess its inability to defend the country; and the Protestant population eagerly seized the opportunity to arm and organize. Soon there had come into being a Volunteer army of Protestant tenantry, shopkeepers, merchants and professional men, under the leadership of the nobility and gentry.

The volunteers, with their highly-coloured uniforms, brass cannons, parades and reviews, dominated the social life of the Anglo-Irish for the next few years. But they did much more: they provided a forum for public opinion. Their military services were not needed—there was no invasion and no fighting—and they were free to turn their attention to politics. They met to discuss the affairs of the kingdom as well as to exercise themselves in arms; and they provided the Patriots in parliament with what they had so far lacked, a national organization. For the first time, the authentic voice of Protestant Ireland, hitherto half strangled in a House of Commons dominated by placemen and hangers-on of government, could find full expression in the free atmosphere of the Volunteer conventions. Ireland's claim to constitutional equality with England took on a new character when supported by 100,000 armed men.

Under pressure of this organized public opinion the House of Commons began to move, though slowly, towards full support for the Patriot programme; and the Whig opposition at Westminster, glad of any weapon with which to attack Lord North, followed the same line. When, in March 1782, North fell and Rockingham came into office, the issue was decided—Ireland was to have, at last, the constitutional rights it had so long demanded.

The so-called 'Constitution of 1782'—in which these rights were enshrined—was at best a ramshackle piece of work. It raised more questions than it decided; and, though the legislative independence of the Irish parliament was established, the Irish executive remained as firmly as ever under the control of the British ministry. Certainly, the sense of victory had a stimulating effect: trade expanded, new industries were established and there was a general rise in prosperity. But the exaggerated hopes that many had nourished were inevitably disappointed: the new Ireland was not very different from the old; the overriding authority of the British ministry seemed as strong and as oppressive as ever; and the Anglo-Irish landlords showed themselves unwilling to share the fruits of their victory with the middle classes who had helped to win it, still less to extend any political power to the Roman Catholic majority. Perhaps things might have developed differently but for the outbreak of the French Revolution, barely seven years after the new constitution had been established. In the political atmosphere created by the Revolution the possibility of gradual and peaceful reform faded away. A few people tried to hold a moderate course; but the field was, in fact, divided between those who were determined to keep things as they were and those who would be satisfied with nothing less than the total overthrow of the existing régime and the setting up of an Irish republic in alliance with France. Out of this conflict sprang the abortive insurrection of 1798, which was followed, almost inevitably, by a parliamentary union with Great Britain; and the 'glorious fabric' of the Constitution of 1782 went down in the wake of a bloody civil war, not twenty years after Grattan had hailed it with his *Esto perpetua*.

(3)

In the course of the nineteenth century, as the Roman Catholic majority made good its claim to be regarded as the Irish nation, the 'Constitution of 1782' and all that went with it took on a new aspect. The Anglo-Irish were now seen as no more than a colonial ruling class, battening on the spoils of conquest and oppressing a native population. The language of Swift and the Patriot leaders was too vigorous to be wholly forgotten, and the suppression of even a Protestant parliament could still be usefully cited an an example of English tyranny; but in popular opinion it was no longer the Protestant Volunteers who represented the true voice of Irish freedom, but the Catholic insurgents of 1798—'The boys of Wexford' celebrated in song and story. If Ireland were indeed to be 'a nation once again', it was certainly not to be the nation of Swift and Grattan.

Looking back across the era in which this concept of 'the Catholic nation' established itself, not only among Irishmen but also among outside observers of the Irish scene, it is difficult to recapture the spirit of the Anglo-Irish of the eighteenth century. The ambiguities and contradictions inherent in their position, which appear so obvious today, seem rarely to have troubled them. However determined they might be to preserve a Protestant ascendancy, however much a long series of conquests and confiscations might have contributed to their estates and their privileges, they saw the history of the Kingdom of Ireland as a continuous process, leading forward to their own supremacy and finding its natural climax in their Constitution of 1782.

Nowhere is this Anglo-Irish interpretation of the past more vividly or more naïvely expressed than in the writings of Sir Jonah Barrington, who was himself a typical representative of the class whose case he defended. The Barringtons had established themselves in Ireland at the end of the sixteenth century and their estates had grown with successive confiscations. Like so many other settler families of the period, they had intermarried both with Old English and with Gaelic Irish, and Sir Jonah had close kindred among the FitzGeralds and the O'Briens. A younger son, with small fortune of his own, he turned to the practice of the law; and, when he entered parliament in 1790, his decision to support government was based frankly on the calculation that this was the course most likely to advance his professional interests. Yet at the same time he was a firm supporter of the constitutional rights of Ireland, rights which he felt to be under the special protection of the landlord class to which he belonged. It is thus that he describes his feelings on taking his seat in the House of Commons: 'I felt myself an entirely independent representative of an equally independent nation—a man assuming his proper station in society, not acquiring a new one.' This boast of independence was not an idle one. Despite his readiness to serve government, and his eagerness in seeking due reward for his services, Barrington regarded the Irish constitution as sacred; and when the proposal for a parliamentary union with Great Britain was brought forward he rejected all inducements to support it, and persisted in an opposition that not only destroyed his prospects of promotion but led to his dismissal from a lucrative sinecure. Once the union had been carried, Barrington accepted it as an unpalatable fact; but he did not change his views about its character, and thirty years later he gave them permanent form in a lively if unreliable book, *The Rise and Fall of the Irish Nation*.

The title of the book, when seen in the light of its subject-matter, provides a perfect illustration of Barrington's outlook: for his theme is, in fact, the history of Irish politics between the winning of the Constitution of 1782 and its destruction by the act of union in 1800. This typically Anglo-Irish view of Irish nationality is given further emphasis in the introductory paragraphs. Here, Barrington traces the oppression of his country to 'the treachery and treasons of MacMurrough', who had first brought English power into Ireland; he dismisses the next six centuries, in a dozen lines, as a time of national apathy; and then plunges at once into his main theme with the assertion that 'it was not until an advanced stage of the American revolt . . . that Ireland began to reflect steadily upon her own deprivations'. For him, there was no break in continuity. England was the enemy in the eighteenth century as in the twelfth; and the Anglo-Irish gentry represented the Irish nation as fully and as truly as the ancient Gaelic monarchies.

Barrington was neither a mature politician nor a deep thinker; and his writings are marked by inaccuracy, prejudice and exaggeration. But on this question of nationality there is no essential difference between his views and those of the more responsible leaders of the Anglo-Irish. They might express themselves less crudely; they might make allowance for changes and developments that Barrington found it convenient to ignore; but they had no doubt that they represented the people of Ireland or that their parliament on College Green was the authentic mouthpiece of an ancient nation. Such beliefs might seem strangely at odds with reality; but people rarely examine the assumptions underlying their attitudes. And the Anglo-Irish had, after all, some ground on which to stand. In an age when property and power went hand in hand, when notions of universal franchise and majority rule had not yet gained currency, when the romantic nationalism of race and language that was to dominate the succeeding age had hardly come to birth, their claim was not so absurd as it seems to us.

This is not to say that the Anglo-Irish themselves were wholly free from uneasiness. Even those of them who were most firmly convinced of their right to represent the national will could hardly overlook the fact that the Protestant population, on whose support they must depend, formed only a small minority of the whole; and some, at least, recognized that to exclude the great bulk of the people from political power, simply on the ground of their religion, produced an anomalous state of affairs. Even Barrington, for all his pride of class and arrogant self-confidence, had no patience with those who raved constantly of the danger to be feared from the papists.

In the long run, it is perhaps by their attitude to the Roman Catholics rather than by their attitude to England that the political outlook of the Anglo-Irish can be most clearly assessed, though the two attitudes are sometimes closely interdependent. Four famous men may be taken as representing different viewpoints: Swift, Grattan, Burke and Tone. All four were educated at Trinity College, with its long tradition of Anglican ascendancy; each sought, in his own way, to forward the interests of Ireland; and each has more than a merely personal significance, for each represents a strand in the Anglo-Irish tradition.

Swift's view was firmly based on his belief in the church and its rights. Ireland was a Protestant kingdom; authority belonged naturally to those who conformed to the church as by law established; and this authority must be preserved, even if it meant excluding the majority of the population from any share of political influence. It was true that the Protestant minority had acquired its position by conquest; but conquest could confer real rights, and the English colonists now in actual possession of the kingdom were entitled to all the freedom that an independent Ireland had once enjoyed, subject only to their allegiance to the crown. Swift was, in fact, determined to have it both ways. Ireland had been added to the dominions of the crown, but as a distinct kingdom, subject to the crown in the same way as England was, but not at all under the authority of the English parliament. At the same time, the English colonists in Ireland were entitled, by virtue of descent, to all the individual and corporate liberties of Englishmen in England. Whatever inconsistencies might lie in this argument, they did not trouble Swift. He might not have claimed that there was no salvation outside the Church of Ireland; but he certainly did claim that those outside should be excluded from any part in the government of the kingdom. 'The whole people of Ireland,' to whom he addressed the fourth of his *Drapier's Letters* and whose cause he so vigorously championed, meant for him the narrow circle of the established church.

It is unlikely that Swift's contemporaries fully understood his views, which he nowhere expressed in a single coherent statement. They have to be pieced together from passages scattered through his writings; and the only element in them which made a clear and lasting impression on the public mind was the assertion that Ireland ought to be treated as a distinct and self-governing kingdom. It was this, certainly, that Grattan had in mind when, in the peroration to his famous Declaration of Independence on 16 April 1782, he invoked the 'Spirit of Swift'. But Grattan would never have accepted Swift's narrow definition of the Irish nation; and he consistently advocated the admission of Roman Catholics to full political rights. This difference between the two men no doubt owed something to change of circumstances: the wars of the Revolution, through which Swift's generation had passed, had now faded into the background. But this is only a partial explanation. Most of Grattan's contemporaries in parliament, including many who had joined in the campaign for independence, retained the old Protestant prejudice almost in its full force; and in advocating a more liberal policy he spoke only for a relatively small minority either in the House of Commons or in the constituencies.

Yet, even here, Grattan could not escape the inner contradiction that seemed inseparable from the Anglo-Irish position. On the one hand, he pressed the political claims of the Roman Catholic majority; on the other, he committed himself to maintaining the Protestant constitution of the kingdom. It is unlikely, indeed, that he ever looked beyond the immediate future. In the Ireland of his day, the state of representation and the distribution of property were such that Roman Catholics, even if admitted to parliament, were unlikely to secure more than a handful of seats; they could present no threat either to the church or to property; and Grattan was prepared to leave the long-term effects to take care of themselves. In all this, as throughout his political career, he was guided by his feelings rather than by any well-considered scheme of action; and he was ready to accept contradictory positions without realizing that a contradiction existed. By ancestry and by conviction he was an upholder of the Anglo-Irish in their claim to be the natural rulers of Ireland; a sense of justice made him champion the rights of the Roman Catholics; but, in his own mind, there was no conflict between the two causes.

When we turn from Swift and Grattan to Burke and Tone we move into a different world. Burke and Tone differed as much in political outlook as they did in quality of mind: but they had at least this in common, that they saw the Irish situation in a wider context than either Swift or Grattan had been willing to recognize. For Swift, the rights of Ireland became important only when he himself was obliged to live there; his assertion of Ireland's equality with England was essentially personal, and expressed, in a different way, the same fierce pride that had earlier characterized his relations with English statesmen. Grattan's outlook was more truly national; but it was bounded by the purpose immediately in hand. He was always more eager to establish principles than ready to consider how they would work out in application. Burke and Tone were more radical and more far-sighted; and it is for this reason that their views, though grounded in the conditions of the eighteenth century, continued to exercise a strong influence in the nineteenth.

Burke's career invites comparison with Swift's. Each, though born and educated in Ireland, moved early to England. Each made his way into political life through his literary work. Each became firmly attached to a party, and established close personal relations with its leaders. But Burke succeeded where Swift had failed: he was able to settle permanently

55

in England, and he became, at least in his own eyes, an Englishman by residence. Swift, in similar circumstances, would almost certainly have put Ireland out of his mind; Burke, though often with apparent reluctance, took a continued interest in Irish affairs, and seems to have felt it his duty to offer guidance, both to the government and to the general public, on matters of policy affecting Ireland. But he never considered Ireland in isolation. The good that he sought was not the good of Ireland for its own sake, but the good of the Empire; and the centre of the Empire was London, its supreme authority the British parliament. Swift, exiled in Dublin, had become the champion of Irish independence; Burke, successfully settled in England, became the champion of English control over Ireland.

In all essentials, the policy that Burke advocated for Ireland was based on this belief in the primacy of imperial interests. His views were sometimes reinforced by personal considerations and occasionally warped by party zeal; but his attitude to Ireland and his conception of the proper relationship between Ireland and England remained remarkably consistent through a period of thirty years. He genuinely desired Irish prosperity, and took a leading part in the successful campaign for the removal of restrictions imposed by the British parliament on Irish trade and industry, even though his conduct eventually cost him his seat at Bristol. But any notion of Irish political independence startled him. Even such a modest reform as the octennial act of 1768, which provided, for the first time, that Ireland should have regular general elections, seemed to him a piece of 'madness', since it would increase the influence of the voters and thus make the House of Commons less responsive to government control. In 1782 he could hardly contain his dismay at the constitutional demands of 'this madman Grattan'. Though party loyalty bridled his opposition and enabled him to swallow the new Irish constitution, he never concealed his dislike of a settlement that, as he put it, took Ireland 'out of the common constitutional protection of the Empire', or, in other words, deprived the British parliament of the right to legislate for Ireland.

In his consistent support for the claims of the Roman Catholics Burke was moved by various influences. His many close connections among them freed him from traditional Protestant prejudice: to him they were not a dangerous or alien enemy, but 'the great body of my original countrymen', 'the ancient people of the country'; and he felt strongly the injustice of excluding them from the rights of citizenship, simply on the grounds of their religion. But the argument to which he returned most often, and on which he laid most stress, was the importance to the Empire of a happy and peaceful Ireland. When at length, in 1793, Roman Catholics were admitted to the parliamentary franchise, his most urgent plea was that this concession should be made 'subservient to the tranquillity of the country and the strength of the Empire'; and his bitterest criticism of the Irish administration of the period—the little group of officials whom he called in contempt the 'Junto' and the 'Click'—was directed against its unwillingness to follow the conciliatory policy that he advocated.

It is entirely typical of Burke's conception of Ireland's status that he did not support the policy of the Irish Whigs, who wished to liberalize the administration through a reform of parliament. His remedy was quite different: it was to deprive the 'Junto' of the substantial independence that it enjoyed and to bring it more closely under the direction of the British ministry. He did not go so far as to recommend a parliamentary union; this was something that he thought should not be attempted, unless 'in some nearly desperate crisis of the Empire'; but, though Ireland might be left with its own parliament, the union at executive level, already existing in form, should be made fully effective and Irish officials deprived of all influence on the formation of policy.

Burke's view of Ireland did not appeal (at least in its entirety) to many among his Anglo-Irish contemporaries. Those who shared his sympathy with the Catholics were for the most part strong supporters of legislative independence; while those who agreed with him on the necessity of Ireland's subordination to Great Britain did so because they regarded this as the surest way of preserving the Protestant ascendancy. But if we extend our view from the eighteenth century to the nineteenth, Burke's place in the Anglo-Irish tradition appears much more representative. When the union had been passed, and when Ireland had been merged with England in the United Kingdom, Burke's concept of the proper relationship between the two countries became, with only slight modification, the orthodoxy of the Anglo-Irish; and few among them would have disagreed with his opinion, expressed in a letter in 1796, that 'Ireland cannot be separated one moment from England without losing every source of her present prosperity and even every hope for her future'. Though they did not, for the most part, share Burke's belief that the Roman Catholics, as a body, were essentially loyal to the British connection, they nevertheless accepted the view that they could no longer be excluded from parliament: Catholic Emancipation was supported by a majority of the Irish members for years before it was eventually passed by the parliament at Westminster. But perhaps there was no way in which the Anglo-Irish of the nineteenth century followed Burke's example so enthusiastically as in devotion to the

imperial idea; and their contribution to the extension, defence and administration of the British Empire was out of all proportion to their numbers.

Swift and Grattan represent the main stream of Anglo-Irish political
thinking in the eighteenth century; Burke, with his view of Ireland as a
dependent but vitally important member of a world-wide Empire, looked
to the future. But where are we to find room in the Anglo-Irish tradition
for Wolfe Tone, who rejected alike the Protestant exclusiveness of Swift,
the parliamentary conservatism of Grattan and the imperialism of Burke,
and who devoted his life to the establishment of an independent and
democratic Irish republic?

But Tone, though he was to become part of the mythology of modern
Irish nationalism, does, in fact, represent a genuine element in the Anglo-
Irish tradition. His early career provides a good example of the fluidity of
Anglo-Irish society. His background was neither aristocratic nor wealthy
—his grandfather was a substantial farmer, his father a coachbuilder; but
he received the education of a gentleman, ate his dinners in the Middle
Temple, and was called to the Irish bar. Thereafter, he had no difficulty in
making his way into good society in Dublin; and a successful career was
open to him had he cared to apply himself to his profession. But he detested
the law, and turned instead to politics. Here, he speedily made the 'great
discovery' (as he calls it) that 'the influence of England was the radical
vice of our government'. But this notion was, as he admits, already
present in the writing of Molyneux and Swift; and if it led him into a
course of action widely different from theirs, the cause of difference is to
be found in the temper and the circumstances of the age. Like so many of
his contemporaries, both in Ireland and in England, he was an enthusiastic
admirer of the French Revolution, and he readily embraced the deistical
philosophy that went with it. His great object now was to establish in
Ireland an independent republic, based on the principles that had over-
thrown church, monarchy and aristocracy in France. And he saw, as the
best means to this end, a union between all sections of the population,
and especially between the two groups who had most cause to complain of
the existing régime, the Protestant dissenters and the Roman Catholics.

Tone was not alone among the Anglo-Irish in advocating these views,
but one of a large group. In the province of Ulster the revolutionary
movement was in the hands of Presbyterian radicals—ministers, merchants and shopkeepers; but elsewhere it was largely inspired and
organized by Anglo-Irish gentry and lawyers. Few of them, it is true, had
Tone's clarity of purpose: some were carried along by a romantic
enthusiasm; some were doctrinaire republicans, with little grasp of the

realities of the situation; some seem almost to have drifted into conspiracy and rebellion, without ever having made a firm decision. But together they formed a substantial body, and their ideas had spread widely through Anglo-Irish society. A contemporary has left an account of a dinner party at Bargay Castle, in County Wexford, in April 1798, and notes that the host and five of his guests, all Protestant gentlemen of standing, were later executed for their share in the insurrection that broke out in the following month.

The war in Wexford, with its stark revelation that Tone's doctrine of unity among Irishmen had done little to curb sectarian passion, checked any further advance of revolutionary enthusiasm among the Anglo-Irish. But the idea that they should provide the leadership for a national movement embracing the whole population did not quite disappear. Though it never attracted more than a tiny group of supporters in any generation, it survived, in one form or another, for more than a century; and it represents an extension, not an abandonment, of the principles enunciated by Molyneux and Swift.

Even among the small group who followed this line, who were ready to abandon privilege and to take their stand along with the majority of their fellow-countrymen, the inner contradiction of the Anglo-Irish position can be traced. It can be found in the career of Tone himself. After he had made his 'great discovery' and had resolved to free Ireland from English control, he could still seek to take his place as a citizen of the Empire. He drew up memoranda for submission to the British ministry proposing the establishment of a colony in the South Seas, with the intention of taking an active part in the project himself; and he was disappointed when his proposals were turned down. Years later, when he was an officer in the French army and awaiting instructions to embark on an invasion of Ireland, he could look back half regretfully on this lost opportunity, and remark, not without a touch of malice, that 'perhaps the minister may yet have reason to wish that he had let us go off quietly to the South Seas'.

This question of political allegiance is less important in itself than as a symptom of underlying uncertainty. The Anglo-Irish were caught between two conflicting influences: Irish by birth and circumstances, they lived in a cultural atmosphere that was essentially English. They could hold the two influences together only by postulating a 'Kingdom of Ireland' that was peculiarly their own. When, as Tone did, they abandoned this concept, and tried to identify themselves with their hereditary enemies, they were left without a firm base on which to stand. For identification was impossible. Tone took up the cause of the Roman Catholics, not because he wished to see their grievances peacefully redressed, but because he hoped to turn their discontent into a revolutionary channel. He used them but he never understood them; and their conviction that to be Irish was to be Roman Catholic was as alien to his way of thought as his notion of a secular state was to theirs.

(4)

The insurrection of 1798 forced the political thinking of the Anglo-Irish into a new mould. The revolutionary minority—Wolfe Tone, Lord Edward FitzGerald, the Sheares brothers and the rest—who had decided for rebellion, separation from England and a French-style republic, saw their plans and hopes crumble in failure. But for the majority the future was still uncertain. In the heat of the insurrection and its aftermath they had been united in defence of their constitution and their property; and perhaps most of them, though certainly not all, wished to exact signal and bloody vengeance: Cornwallis, the newly appointed lord lieutenant, complained that the talk at his dinner table ran on nothing but hanging and shooting. But rebellion, though crushed, had created a new state of affairs, not only in Ireland but in Britain. Pitt was now convinced that the only hope of peace and conciliation lay in abolishing the Constitution of 1782 and merging Ireland with Great Britain in a new 'United Kingdom' under the parliament of Westminster, enlarged by the inclusion of Irish members. This was the issue that the Anglo-Irish now had to face; and it produced among them a division of opinion that ran through all ranks of society, from the peer in parliament to the weaver in his workshop.

The story of the union has been told so often that it need not be told again here; but it is necessary to disentangle some relevant elements from the confusion created by the heat of controversy and the prejudice of historians. The fact that the government employed all the resources of parliamentary 'management' in order to create a favourable majority in the House of Commons must not blind us to the existence of a large body of genuine support for union, both in parliament and in the country. The weight of oratory was on the side of the anti-unionists; and the theme of national independence provided more opportunity for picturesque declamation than the speculative advantages of union. Grattan, in his Volunteer uniform, risen from a bed of sickness to defend the freedom of his country, is a more romantic figure than the cold and calculating Castlereagh, offering titles in exchange for votes. But the anti-unionists, for all their eloquence, had no coherent policy. They could not agree among themselves on any remedy for the desperate ills of the country and their attitude was wholly negative.

This struggle over the union has, in retrospect, an air of unreality; not so much because the power of the government to create a majority was, in the circumstances, irresistible, as because the Anglo-Irish themselves were in the last resort disputing over means rather than ends. What they wanted above all else was to retain their own supremacy in Ireland; and the issue before them might be reduced to the simple question: Could that supremacy best be secured by parliamentary union or by parliamentary independence? There were, it is true, some on both sides who were prepared to complete the political emancipation of the Roman Catholics by admitting them to parliament: on this point Grattan and Castlereagh were in agreement. But neither they, nor those who supported them, had any notion of majority rule. They saw the Roman Catholic nobility and gentry, who would be the immediate beneficiaries of emancipation, as potential allies in the battle against revolutionary France and against French ideas in Ireland. The great bulk of the Anglo-Irish, however, had been so shaken by the dangers through which they had just passed that they thought of little beyond the defence of their own privileged position.

Nowhere is this attitude more evident than among the rank and file of the Orange Societies. These had taken their rise in the 1790s among the Protestant tenantry of County Armagh, but had soon spread to other classes of society and other parts of the country, with the declared purpose of maintaining the Protestant ascendancy. The numerous gentry who joined the movement were easily able to acquire a dominant place in its central organization; and on the question of union they were amenable to government influence. But they found it impossible to control the membership in general; and outside Dublin some of the loudest and fiercest opposition to union came from Protestant farmers and linen-weavers, who saw in the destruction of the Irish parliament the removal of a protective barrier against the power of the Roman Catholic majority.

The Orangemen's confidence in the ability of Irish Protestants to defend their own supremacy had been strengthened by the part played by the yeomanry in defeating the insurrection; for this force, unlike the militia, was almost wholly Protestant and was dominated by Orange influence. The soundness of this judgement was hotly debated in parliament as well as in the country; and the debate helps to clarify the real issue at stake. In the long run, the most compelling argument in favour of union was that Protestant Ireland depended, and always must depend, on military support from Britain, and that only by union could the continuance of that support be guaranteed. This line, naturally followed by the unionists, was countered by the assertion that the gentlemen of Ireland and their loyal tenants, whether in the militia or the yeomanry, had themselves broken the insurrection before reinforcements from Britain had arrived. In one way, the debate was academic, since the government majority in parliament depended on the force of patronage rather than the force of argument; but it serves to bring out clearly the sense of danger that pervaded the whole Anglo-Irish community from top to bottom. And this sense of danger did not arise merely from the state of Ireland, but also from the state of Europe. With the collapse of the Second Coalition the whole continent seemed to lie open to French arms and influence; Britain was left to continue the struggle on her own; and the Anglo-Irish, whatever side they took in the controversy over union, were profoundly aware that Britain's fate in the struggle would be their fate also. It is impossible to tell how far this consideration influenced men's attitudes to union; but it certainly strengthened the feeling of solidarity with Britain, as against France, a feeling that was shared even by the strongest defenders of the rights of the Irish parliament. When the union had been carried and when the heat of controversy had died down, this sense of solidarity survived.

With the union, the Kingdom of Ireland came to an end; and the Anglo-Irish, deprived of the constitutional framework that had given meaning to their existence as a community, could no longer claim to be the Irish nation. But they had, as they always had had, an alternative nationality at hand. Though it is unlikely that they were directly influenced by Burke's teaching, they were willing to follow his example and accept, even if they had originally opposed, the merging of Ireland in the Empire. Yet the tradition of centuries could not be extinguished overnight; and the Anglo-Irish never completely lost their sense of distinctiveness, not only from the majority in their own country, with whom they had so often been in conflict, but also from the English, with whom they mingled so easily and whose battles they were ever ready to fight.

IV

The Eighteenth-century Achievement

(1)

The course of Irish history since the act of union has made it difficult to assess the eighteenth century fairly. The triumphant emergence of a Catholic and Gaelic nationalism has changed the outlook and modified the judgement even of those who find it uncongenial. Today, the politics of College Green seem remote and irrelevant, the very notion of Protestant ascendancy a self-confessed negation of natural justice. For many Irishmen, perhaps for most, the eighteenth century is a kind of hiatus in the life of the nation, a valley of humiliation between the failure of national aspirations in the Jacobite war and their revival more than a hundred years later. And during this dark period the true Ireland was not the Ireland of the Protestant oppressor, but the exiled Ireland of the Wild Geese or the 'hidden Ireland' of the Gaelic-speaking peasantry.

Yet if we free ourselves, as well as we can, from the presuppositions of a later age, and try to look at the eighteenth century as it really was, we see a somewhat different picture. Between the 1690s and the 1790s Ireland had a longer period of internal peace and security than ever before or since. Though there was a good deal of rural disorder, it was local in its incidence, social and economic in origin and aim. Agrarian agitators —Whiteboys, Oakboys, Steelboys—directed their attacks against land-lord and tithe-collector, not against the state. Those who claimed to represent the Catholic majority were loud in their profession of loyalty to the crown; and so far were they from seeking to overthrow the existing constitution that their chief aim was to be allowed to share more fully in its benefits. Until the importation of French ideas at the very end of the period, there was no sign of any political move against the established framework of government. The Kingdom of Ireland, whose rights the Volunteers so strongly asserted, was the only Ireland known to the eighteenth-century world; and it was the Ireland of the Protestant ascendancy.

In Ireland, as in many other parts of contemporary Europe, political power was in the hands of the landlord class. But it would be a mistake (though a mistake not uncommonly made) to assume that Protestant Ireland consisted only, or mainly, of landlords. Protestants, though only a minority of the whole population, made up a substantial body, embracing all ranks of society. Actual numbers are a matter of dispute; but proportions can be calculated with some approach to accuracy. Sir William Petty, in 1670, put the population of Ireland at 1,100,000, of whom 300,000 were Protestants. An estimate of the 1730s, based on the hearth-money returns, gives the same proportion of Protestants to Roman Catholics, that is, three to eight. If we assume that the hearth-money returns were incomplete, which they certainly were, and that the majority of the dwellings omitted were small cabins, most probably inhabited by Roman Catholics, we may not unreasonably assume that the Protestant population amounted to about one-fourth of the whole.

The geographical distribution of Protestants was very uneven. They were weak in Connaught, somewhat stronger in Munster, stronger still in Leinster, especially in Dublin, where they probably accounted for about half the population of the city. But their main concentration was in Ulster, where they outnumbered the Roman Catholics, though the margin of difference was probably not very great. Ulster Protestants were, however, divided among themselves: a large proportion, probably more than half, were of Scottish Presbyterian extraction and dissenters from the established church. This Scottish and Presbyterian element gave a special character to Ulster life; but it was not until a later period, when landlord power was in decline, when the church had been disestablished, and when democratic reform had given more weight to Presbyterian numbers, that the full political significance of the difference between Ulster and the rest of Protestant Ireland was clearly revealed. In the eighteenth century, the Ulster Presbyterians, though they suffered some deprivations on account of their nonconformity, formed part of the 'Protestant nation' and thought of themselves as Irishmen. And they contributed increasingly, as the century progressed, to the formation of a Protestant popular opinion that the House of Commons, however unrepresentative it might be, could not altogether ignore.

Even if the direct political influence of rank-and-file Protestants was small, it was they who made the maintenance of Protestant ascendancy possible. For one thing, they provided a reservoir of military strength. A muster of the militia, taken in the 1750s, showed 150,000 Protestants capable of bearing arms. Some forty years later, the yeomanry—an almost wholly Protestant force, recruited mainly among the better-off tenantry—numbered more than 50,000 men, and it was regarded by many

Protestants as their best protection against a possible 'popish terror'. Again, a substantial body of Protestants was necessary for the proper functioning of local government: it was notoriously in those areas where the Protestant population was weakest that local government was least effective. In short, the position and power of the landlords would have been precarious, and probably untenable, had they not had behind them a large body of lower- and middle-class Protestants.

This interdependence of classes may have contributed to the degree of fluidity that marked Anglo-Irish society. Irish Protestants, however much they differed in economic and social status, had a common sense of superiority to the Roman Catholics and of the need to stand together against them in an emergency. This situation tended to produce among Protestants a kind of aristocratic egalitarianism: since it was generally safe to assume that an Irish gentleman was a Protestant, there was a temptation to reverse the order and assume that an Irish Protestant was a gentleman. At the very least, there was no insuperable barrier to prevent a poor Protestant from climbing the social ladder. William Conolly started life in total obscurity—his father, according to common report, was either a blacksmith or a publican; but he rose to wealth and eminence, married the sister of an earl and became Speaker of the House of Commons. Patrick Delaney, the friend of Swift and one of the leading social figures in Dublin, was the son of a small farmer. Richard Baldwin, provost of Trinity College, came from a background so humble and obscure that conflicting stories give different accounts of his parentage; but all agree that he was a homeless child, educated out of charity. Charles Lucas, a radical agitator who became M.P. for the city of Dublin, was brought up in poverty and apprenticed to an apothecary. Such striking changes of fortune were comparatively rare; but a more modest movement of individuals, and of families, up the social scale occurred frequently enough to strengthen the natural coherence of the Protestant community. And the very possibility of such advancement was an essential characteristic of the ascendancy: a Protestant boy, however humble his origin, might hope to rise, by some combination of ability, good luck and patronage, to a position of influence from which a Roman Catholic, however well-born or wealthy, would be utterly excluded.

It was, then, the Protestants as a body, and not just the landlords, who dominated Ireland in the eighteenth century. Whether one regards them as oppressors or patriots, as alien intruders or genuine Irishmen, they left an enduring mark on the country and its people, and not least on those who were to be their strongest critics. What the Protestant ascendancy accomplished in the day of its power, and what it left behind of good or evil, form an integral part of Ireland's past and contribute to its present.

(2)

A visitor to Ireland at the present day, seeking to recapture the spirit of the eighteenth-century Anglo-Irish, would find their most striking achievement in architecture, in the country houses, large and small, the city squares, the public buildings, that still stand as memorials to their wealth, their taste and their sense of power and security. The most striking example of this architectural heritage is, naturally, the city of Dublin. Its very existence as a capital is an expression of that overflow of English power into Ireland of which the Anglo-Irish were the product. There is nothing Gaelic about Dublin except its name. The Norsemen founded it; the English made it a capital for the whole country; the Anglo-Irish gave it the character that it still retains, despite gradual erosion by the social and economic needs of a twentieth-century republic that has little respect and less love for the Protestant ascendancy of the eighteenth century.

The beginnings of modern Dublin date from the Restoration period, and thus coincide with the clear emergence of Anglo-Irish supremacy. In 1660 the city already stretched far beyond its medieval walls; but development had been haphazard, the streets were narrow and there were few distinguished buildings. Of the two cathedrals, Christ Church was half ruinous and St. Patrick's very much in need of repair. The Castle, though it contained a few fine apartments, had little to commend it externally. Trinity College was still housed in its modest Elizabethan quadrangle. Nearby, on Hoggen Green (later to be known as College Green), a few of the nobility had built their town houses; and one of these, Chichester House, was the usual meeting-place of parliament. In all this, there was little to suggest the dignity of a capital. So, at least, thought the duke of Ormond when he took up office as lord lieutenant in 1662; and he determined to initiate a change. It seems entirely appropriate that Ormond, whose own career embodied the transition from 'Old English' to 'Anglo-Irish' should have presided over the first stage in the development of medieval Dublin into the Anglo-Irish city that it was to become in the next century.

Though Ormond's ambitions for Dublin were shared and forwarded by the corporation of the city, the Restoration period proved to be one of preparation rather than achievement; and it has left behind only one distinguished building, the Royal Hospital at Kilmainham. But it was at this time that the lines of future development were determined; and already, before the Revolution, the framework of the Georgian city that was to be the political, social and intellectual centre of eighteenth-century Ireland had begun to appear. When the Revolutionary wars had re-established and strengthened Protestant supremacy, expansion went on apace.

The architect whose name is most commonly associated with Georgian Dublin was an Englishman, James Gandon. But Gandon's work belongs to the very end of the period, when the architectural character of Dublin had already been established. The men who contributed most to the establishment of that character, during the first few decades after the Revolution, were Thomas Burgh and Edward Lovett Pearce; and both came from typically Anglo-Irish backgrounds. Burgh, who may fairly be regarded as the first distinctively Irish architect, was a descendant of the de Burgo family, which had at one time dominated Connaught, and his father, Ulysses Burgh, had been bishop of Ardagh. Pearce was the grandson of a lord mayor of Dublin and was related, through his mother, to the O'Moores of Leix. Between them they were responsible for most of the best architectural work in the city during the forty years that followed the Revolution; and each is particularly associated with a famous building. Burgh designed the library of Trinity College and Pearce the new parliament house, begun in 1729. In the later 1720s these two were joined by Richard Castle (or Cassels), a German architect who had originally been brought to Ireland by Sir Gustavus Hume, for whom he designed a mansion on the shores of Lough Erne. He subsequently settled in Dublin, where he designed many of the town houses, in cut stone, that the nobility had begun to build. But he did not work only for the nobility and the wealthy land-owners; he designed many more modest houses also; and his style had considerable influence on both contemporaries and successors. When he died, in 1751, the outward appearance of Dublin was very different from what it had been when King William's victorious army marched into the city after the battle of the Boyne.

Of these three architects, only one, Burgh, is known to have designed a church. But there was, in fact, a good deal of church-building during the period; and, as in London, part of the cost was met from funds voted by parliament. By 1730 at least six new churches had been built, and some older churches had been reconstructed and enlarged. The building of new churches reflected the territorial expansion of the city; but the fact that most of them were provided with galleries, usually occupied by the humbler part of the congregation, shows that there was expansion of the church-going population also, and not only among the well-to-do classes. The Protestant character of eighteenth-century Dublin did not depend simply on a small ruling class. It rested firmly on a large Protestant body, comprising perhaps half the total population and running through all ranks of society, though stronger among the well-to-do and the skilled workers than among the very poor.

In the latter half of the century the growing prosperity of Ireland was naturally reflected in the capital. The substantial middle class of well-to-do merchants and professional men, always an important element in the Dublin population, grew both in numbers and influence; and it was to meet the demand of this class for larger and more imposing houses that new streets and squares were laid out. It is the cumulative effect of this domestic architecture, concentrated in a relatively small area, rather than the distinction of individual public buildings, that gave Georgian Dublin its character. In the restrained dignity and quiet confidence of these rows of red-brick houses we can sense the spirit of the Protestant ascendancy far more intimately than in the country houses of the aristocracy or the public splendour of the Custom House and the Four Courts.

These two buildings, often regarded as the chief glories of Dublin architecture, belong to the closing decades of the century, when the Anglo-Irish, then at the height of their power and independence, were determined to adorn their capital city in a manner worthy of the splendid future to which they looked forward; and both were the work of the same architect, James Gandon. The person chiefly responsible for bringing him to Dublin, as architect of the new Custom House, was John Beresford, first commissioner of the revenue and a man of such wide-ranging influence that he was sometimes called, in derision or envy, the 'king of Ireland'. As a politician, Beresford has been much maligned; but his choice of Gandon for this work, the most important architectural undertaking in Dublin since the building of the parliament house half a century earlier, shows that he must have had considerable perspicacity in matters of taste. Gandon, it is true, had already made a respectable reputation, based partly on his books; but he had never before been entrusted with a work on anything like the scale of the Dublin Custom House. His performance fully justified Beresford's choice; and when, a few years later, the decision was taken to rebuild the old Four Courts, it was natural that this task also should be entrusted to Gandon. Together, these two buildings form a splendid memorial to the genius of the architect who designed them and to the good taste and large ideas of the men who governed the Kingdom of Ireland in the eighteenth century.

The wealth and taste so abundantly displayed in Georgian Dublin were not confined to the capital; they have left their memorials in every part of the country. The eighteenth century brought with it peace and a new sense of security. The recurrent warfare that had discouraged any building save for purpose of defence now seemed a thing of the past; for the first time, the Irish gentry could afford to design their houses with an eye to elegance and comfort, and they were not slow to use the opportunity. When, in the late 1720s, Sir Gustavus Hume decided to rebuild his family mansion and brought over Richard Castle to assist him, he was following a fashion that had already been set. Most of the building during the first decades of the century was on a comparatively modest scale; but in 1722 work had begun on the first of the great Georgian country houses, Castletown, in County Kildare. It was built for William Conolly, whose career is a useful reminder that even in the aristocratic eighteenth century the road to power and wealth was open to men of ability as well as to men of birth. When Castletown House was built he was reputedly the richest commoner in the country; but Castletown is a memorial to his taste as well as to his wealth, for he himself took an active part in designing it. George Berkeley, whose advice he sought, goes so far as to say that the plan of the house was 'chiefly of Mr. Conolly's invention' and that its detailed execution was supervised by a kind of committee made up of Conolly and some of his friends. Berkeley probably exaggerated; but what emerges clearly enough is that Conolly and his colleagues were men of sufficient taste and knowledge to have a real influence on the work. They must, presumably, have had the assistance of a professional architect; but of this there is no direct evidence. Modern experts are inclined to divide the credit between Burgh and Pearce; if they are right, Castletown House—perhaps the most splendid example of domestic architecture in the whole country, and one of the finest in the three kingdoms—is a distinctively Anglo-Irish achievement.

There are only a few country houses of the period built on the same magnificent scale as Castletown; and these few can all be assigned to particular architects. But there are scores of smaller houses about whose origins we know little or nothing. Conolly was certainly not unique in planning a house for himself. Many another country gentleman, of less distinction and smaller means, was content to act as his own architect, relying, perhaps, on Batty Langley's *Sure Guide to Builders* or, later in the century, on John Plaw's *Rural Architecture*; and the actual work would be entrusted to local craftsmen. Langley's book was published in 1729; but more than ten years earlier we find Kean O'Hara, a County Sligo landlord of modest fortune, designing his own house at Collooney. Like Conolly, he consulted his friends; and one of them, while giving general approval to the plan of the house, offered some criticism: 'The roof you have fixed upon will make it look very mean, so you must alter your design in that.' Meanness was certainly not a common failing of these amateur architects. The houses they designed are often plain enough; but the prevalent good taste is revealed in their proportions; and they achieve, at the least, a sober dignity that seems oddly at variance with the traditional picture of the swaggering, drunken, illiterate Irish squire.

The very number of country houses built during the period is significant. The Georgian Society's volume on country houses lists over two hundred and seventy, but indicates that the total must be very much greater: partly because most of the smaller houses (perhaps amounting to some hundreds) have been omitted; partly because many houses originally Georgian in style were later altered or rebuilt to suit the new fashions of the nineteenth century. With so many country houses, large and small, in every part of the kingdom, it is hard not to believe that the number of landlords who lived on their estates, for part of the year at least, was larger than their critics have commonly been willing to allow. But the argument must not be pressed too far: even a landlord who rarely or never resided might yet feel it his duty to build and maintain a house on the estate. The 'Big House'—to use the term current in rural Ireland—was not just a dwelling-place, it was a symbol; and for the landlords in general it gave outward expression to their power, their status and their sense of permanence. They misjudged the future; the trend of political and social development was against them; and today not many of these houses are still the homes of the families that built them. Some are derelict. Some are schools, convents or monasteries. Many were burnt out in the 1920s as a warning to the occupants that they were not wanted in the new Ireland that was emerging.

The quiet dignity that was characteristic of these country houses can be found also in many of the provincial cities and towns. At the beginning of the eighteenth century they were, for the most part, small and poor, with little to boast of in their appearance. Some still showed the remnants of medieval importance as military and ecclesiastical centres: mouldering walls, dilapidated castles, ruinous churches and monasteries. Except in a few seaports, the general impression was one of poverty and decay. But as the country became more prosperous urban life quickened and the appearance of the towns improved; Arthur Young, writing in the 1770s, could declare that 'Ireland has been absolutely new-built within these twenty years'.

Cork is a striking example of this development. Its importance was based on the export of provisions, which increased steadily during the century; and its merchants were among the wealthiest in the kingdom. They built handsome houses for themselves and they sought to improve the appearance and the amenities of their city. They built bridges, widened the streets and laid out the Mardyke, the South Mall and the Grand Parade. They provided public buildings: the Exchange, the Corn Market, the Mansion House. They rebuilt the ancient cathedral in the prevailing classical style and they built new churches to meet the needs of the growing population, for Cork, like Dublin, had a large body of Protestants. By the end of the century, Cork was one of the busiest and handsomest seaport towns in the British Isles.

For other provincial towns also, the eighteenth century was a period of growth, though none of them could equal Cork in wealth or size. Where, as not infrequently happened, a town was the property of a single landlord, little could be done without his co-operation; but in such cases it was commonly the landlord himself who took the initiative in development. At Newtownards, for example, the Stewart family did much to improve the town and built, in 1770, the graceful market-house that still dominates the central square. Fermoy, in County Cork, was transformed in the space of a few years from a group of miserable cabins into a well-built and prosperous town simply by the energy and foresight of a new land-lord. The ancient but dilapidated city of Armagh was virtually rebuilt in the course of the century under the direction of successive primates, but especially under Richard Robinson, who held the see from 1765 to 1795. He repaired and beautified the cathedral; he built an archiepiscopal palace and houses for the vicars choral; he provided the city with a public library and an observatory, both generously endowed; he bequeathed funds for the establishment of a university, though this project was never carried out. Belfast, like Cork, was growing largely in wealth; and the inhabitants were anxious to improve their town. But they could have achieved little without the co-operation of the earls of Donegall, who owned the land on which it was built. Fortunately for the townspeople, the fifth earl, who succeeded to the title in 1765, was an enthusiastic improver. He granted new leases to promote an orderly development, in which he himself invested large sums. The elegance and dignity that the town acquired under his guidance were to be swamped by the rapid and uncontrolled expansion of the next century; but the lay-out of the streets round the modern City Hall gives some idea of what Belfast might have become if the spirit of an earlier age had survived.

These examples might be multiplied many times over. Irish urban architecture is, for the most part, undistinguished; but there are few towns of any note that have not some remnants, at the least, of eighteenth-century good taste—a church, a market-house, an old school, a street façade. And very often this is the only thing that relieves the general drabness; unless, perhaps, there is the ruin of some ancient castle or monastery. Generally speaking, indeed, the only architectural features that give pleasure to the eye or stir the imagination are the creation of either the Anglo-Norman settlers of the medieval period or their Anglo-Irish successors of the eighteenth century.

(3)

Country mansions, public buildings, urban development—all alike reflected an improvement in the national economy. The wealth that resulted from this improvement was very unequally distributed, and throughout most of the country there were still ample indications of poverty: much of the rural population was housed in wretched one-room cabins, and every town had its swarm of beggars. But the gloomy picture drawn by many contemporaries, and often copied by historians, is unduly dark. The close connection between Ireland and England has made it natural to judge Ireland by English standards; and, in comparison with England, Ireland was still a poor and backward country. But in comparison with its own past, and in comparison with many parts of Europe, eighteenth-century Ireland was notable for its economic progress.

During the hundred years that followed the Revolution population grew, agricultural production increased, old industries expanded and new ones were established. There was, in consequence, a great development of trade; in 1701 the total value of exports had been less than seven hundred thousand pounds; by the 1770s the value of linen exports alone had risen to almost two millions; and during the same interval the exports of beef, pork and butter were very nearly tripled. As a result, landlords were able to raise their rents; merchants and manufacturers increased in number and wealth; bankers and lawyers found more scope and made greater profits; even the parochial clergy benefited, for the value of tithe rose with agricultural improvement. These groups together constituted the upper layer of Irish society and determined its character. It was they who dominated the life of Dublin and of the provincial cities and towns; it was they who conducted local administration; and from their ranks were drawn the members of both Houses of Parliament.

This upper layer of society was not exclusively Protestant or exclusively Anglo-Irish. There were some Roman Catholics among the landlords, though their number declined in the course of the century as more and more conformed under pressure of the penal laws. There were a good many Roman Catholic merchants, some of them very wealthy; but they were totally excluded from any political power. Among both merchants and manufacturers, especially in the province of Ulster, there was a substantial body of Protestant dissenters, mainly of Scottish extraction, who exercised a good deal of local influence. Yet, despite these exceptions, the typical member of upper-class society was also a member of the established church—the Church of Ireland—which was the most characteristic embodiment of the Anglo-Irish tradition. And this church tended to gather in not only Roman Catholics anxious to escape the restrictions imposed by the penal laws but also wealthy Protestant dissenters, and more especially those who had purchased land in the hope of raising their social status. Men who conformed from such motives were unlikely to make sincere churchmen, nor did they always abandon their former connections or inherited ways of thought. But the case was different with their children and grandchildren, who received the benefits of the change without enduring its hardships. They enlarged and enriched the Anglo-Irish community without diluting its essential character; and in the next century some of the most earnest clergy of the Church of Ireland, as well as some of its strongest political defenders, came from families which had changed their faith primarily for material advantage.

In the traditional and generally accepted picture of this eighteenth-century Anglo-Irish society the most familiar figure is the greedy and tyrannical landlord, squeezing the last penny of rent out of a starving tenantry and spending the proceeds in the fashionable world of London and Bath or in riotous living at home. No doubt there were many such landlords; and they may well have been commoner in Ireland than in contemporary England. But they certainly did not make up the whole of Irish society, nor were they the most influential element in it. Their strongest critics, in their own day, were to be found among their fellow-Irishmen of the same social class; and it is largely on the evidence of these critics that the accepted picture is based. Irish society was tolerant of extravagance, believed in lavish hospitality, without much regard to the means by which it was supported, and admired physical prowess. But these were not its only standards of judgement: it had, also, a clear sense of public and national duty; though in Ireland, as elsewhere, this was commonly stronger in principle than in practice. It is worth remembering that one of the very few plays depicting Irish life to achieve lasting popularity in eighteenth-century Ireland was Charles Macklin's *True-born Irishman*, in which the hero is a landlord who lives at home, improves his estate, looks after his tenants and dissuades his wife from squandering money on imported luxuries. The spectators in the theatres of Dublin or Cork or Limerick who regularly applauded these expressions of practical patriotism represented a fair cross-section of the Protestant ascendancy that is so often identified with the follies and vices that Macklin set out to expose.

Macklin's play is now almost forgotten except by historians of the drama; but other delineations of eighteenth-century society have proved more enduring, and two writers, in particular, have had a good deal of influence in the formation of later opinion—Sir Jonah Barrington and Maria Edgeworth. Both have been, in some measure, misunderstood. Barrington's *Personal Sketches of His Own Times* was never intended as a serious portrayal of social conditions. It was, as he tells us himself, a 'desultory *mélange*' of his recollections, put together for amusement. This does not mean that the book has no value for the historian: used with discrimination it can enlarge our understanding of the period. But its emphasis on the bizarre and the eccentric—a natural consequence of the author's purpose—has often misled careless readers into supposing that these are the essential characteristics of Anglo-Irish life, though Barrington's own career, both in law and politics, is clear evidence to the contrary.

Barrington, in his *Personal Sketches*, wrote to entertain, Maria Edgeworth wrote not only to entertain but also to inform and instruct; and her two novels of eighteenth-century Ireland were intended to provide a true picture of rural conditions. It should, however, be remembered that she was writing about the life of an earlier period, for which she had to rely upon the recollections of other people rather than upon her own observation. *Castle Rackrent*, published in 1801, and *Ormond*, published in 1817, were historical novels, not tales of contemporary life, or even of very recent times: 'the race of the Rackrents', wrote Miss Edgeworth, in the preface to *Castle Rackrent*, 'has long been extinct in Ireland.' This historical character of the novels does not impair their value as evidence:

Miss Edgeworth was well versed in rural traditions and able to enter thoroughly into the spirit of an earlier generation; but it is important to bear in mind that the picture she drew is not meant to be applicable to the whole century. It is hardly less important that she was writing for an English public, and therefore tended to emphasize those aspects of the scene that appeared to her to be peculiarly Irish; and, generally speaking, it is these aspects that remain most vividly in the reader's mind. The result is that these novels, despite the author's care, have helped to propagate a somewhat unbalanced picture of Anglo-Irish society in the eighteenth century. The fault is not with Miss Edgeworth; and perhaps it is hardly fair to blame the reader either—what appears absurd or grotesque is always more memorable than the familiar. Readers have been very much inclined to take for granted those characters whose behaviour conforms to 'English' standards and concentrate their attention on the others: they remember King Corny long after they have forgotten Lady Annaly and her family.

But the Annalys ought not to be forgotten. They represent an important element in Anglo-Irish society, and one without which Ireland would have been a very different place. Their high sense of duty, their constant concern for the welfare of the tenantry, their interest in literature—all reflected the kind of life that Miss Edgeworth herself lived with her father at Edgeworthstown; and in every level of society there were many families guided by similar principles, though comparatively few of them had abilities or means equal to those of the Annalys, in fiction, or the Edgeworths, in real life. The importance of such people did not lie simply in what they could accomplish on their own estates or in their own localities. It was they who provided the stimulus and leadership for corporate efforts to improve social conditions and promote economic development throughout the country as a whole; and their example attracted the support of many who would otherwise have been content to let things drift.

By far the most important of these corporate undertakings was the Dublin Society, founded in 1731 to promote agriculture, manufactures and the useful arts. It started in a small way; but it reflected a widespread conviction that something must be done to improve the Irish economy. The most memorable and most forceful expression of this conviction is to be found in the pamphlets of Swift; but there were many writers of less note who taught the same lesson: Thomas Prior, the main agent in the foundation of the Dublin Society, had himself published a *List of the Absentees of Ireland,* in which he calculated the amount lost to the country annually by payments to absentee landlords, office-holders and pensioners. When he and a handful of friends launched their scheme in the summer of 1731 the way had at least been prepared; but success must depend upon sustained and well-directed effort. For almost two decades the Society had to rely entirely on voluntary subscriptions; and it was its achievement during this period that won the support of parliament in 1749, thus setting the Society on a firmer financial basis.

A brief account of some of Prior's principal colleagues in these early years of the Society will indicate the kind of people involved. Sir Thomas Molyneux belonged to a family that had been settled in Ireland since the sixteenth century, and whose members had held lucrative posts under the crown; but his own considerable income was derived from his practice as a physician in Dublin. Francis Bindon, the son of a Limerick citizen, was an architect and a popular portrait painter. George Faulkner was the son of a victualler, who became the most famous of Dublin printers and booksellers. Henry Brooke, the son of a country parson and minor land-owner, was a lawyer by profession, but is best remembered as a pamphlet-eer, poet and novelist. Of the many clergy who supported the Society three may be taken as samples. Patrick Delaney, a man of humble origins, had risen by his own ability and Swift's patronage to be dean of Down. Thomas Sheridan, another friend of Swift's, obtained little professional advancement, but acquired an estate in County Cavan by marriage. Samuel Madden, the son of a Dublin medical practitioner who was also a landowner, is remembered both for his generous benefactions and for his influential pamphlet, *Reflections and Resolutions Proper for the Gentlemen of Ireland*; but in his own day he had also a considerable reputation as dramatist and poet. Here, then, in the early membership of the Dublin Society, we have a fair cross-section of what might reasonably be regarded as the most important element in the Anglo-Irish tradition. Public attention has most commonly been fastened on the absentee noble or the swashbuckling squireen; but if we are to find the true character of Anglo-Irish life we must seek it in the middle ranks of society, among merchants and professional men, who might often, indeed, have links with the land-owning class, but whose influence in the world depended on ability and initiative rather than on wealth.

The Dublin Society was one of the first institutions of its kind in Europe, and proved to be one of the most successful. Much of its attention was devoted to agriculture, which was by far the most important of the country's industries: it set up a model farm, provided instruction, encouraged tillage, imported and distributed better implements than those in general use. But it was concerned also to promote manufactures, so as to diversify the economy, make Ireland less dependent on imported goods and create more opportunities for employment. The encouragement of the useful arts, to which the Society was committed by its original programme, was not neglected. It took over a private drawing-school, established by Robert West, a well-known Dublin painter, retaining West's services as master. A few years later this was extended by the addition of an architectural section, under the guidance of Thomas Ivory, who was later to be the architect of one of the most attractive Dublin buildings of the century, the Blue-coat School. Ivory had been born in Cork, in humble circumstances—it is said that he began life as a carpenter —and had worked his way up, by his own ability and efforts, to become one of the most distinguished architects in the capital. He may fairly be regarded as a specimen, though a peculiarly favourable specimen, of the kind of talent that the Society hoped to encourage; and, in order that this encouragement might be spread as widely as possible, no fees were charged for attendance at the classes it provided. Some, at least, of the credit for the good quality of much Irish building in the latter half of the century may fairly be attributed to this generosity: apprentices to the building trade in the Dublin area commonly received part of their instruction in the Society's school; and, through them, its influence spread to other parts of the kingdom.

The Dublin Society must not be seen in isolation. It had no monopoly of good intentions; and there were many people in all parts of the country who worked for similar ends, whether in groups or as individuals. But the Dublin Society, because of its central position, the ability of its leaders and its resources, was particularly influential, not only through what it accomplished itself, but also by the example it set. It was, however, an organizing rather than a creative force: its schemes for the development of the economy contained nothing new in principle; and in its work for the arts it reflected taste rather than guided it. The Society's schools encouraged a high standard of craftsmanship; but the good taste that informs the silverwork, the furniture, the glassware, the book-bindings of the period owes a great deal to the discriminating judgement of the public that the craftsmen served.

(4)

The essential concern of the Dublin Society was to promote the advancement of useful knowledge, to disseminate it as widely as possible and to encourage its application to the various branches of industry. But, side by side with this utilitarian outlook, there existed among the Anglo-Irish another, and older, tradition of pursuing knowledge for its own sake. The two traditions were not, of course, mutually exclusive; and many of those who supported the Dublin Society were just as much interested in natural philosophy, in classical learning, in history and antiquities, as they were in the more practical subjects on which the Society, as a body, concentrated its attention. Sir Thomas Molyneux, one of Prior's most useful supporters in the foundation of the Society, provides a good example of this diversity of interests. He had been a member of an earlier body, the Dublin Philosophical Society, founded in 1684 in imitation of the Royal Society in England. A few years later this Society perished in the Revolution and it was never re-established; but several of its members remained active in the intellectual life of Ireland for a long time, though very few of them for so long as Sir Thomas Molyneux. Over a period of almost fifty years he continued to publish papers, not only on medical science (in which, as a physician, he was professionally concerned) but on zoology, on natural phenomena, on classical and Irish antiquities, on the principles of taxation. This represents a range of interest commoner in the seventeenth century than in the eighteenth; but there were many of his contemporaries and successors whose concern for economic and social improvement was combined with an active interest in learning, literature and the fine arts.

For the greater part of the century, however, such people had neither any regular meeting-place nor any continuing organization. Groups and coteries were formed from time to time; but the need for some permanent and formal body remained until 1785, when a meeting held in Charlemont House, the town residence of Lord Charlemont, resolved to set up an Irish Academy and elected Charlemont as its first president. It was his influence that obtained for the Academy, early in the following year, a royal charter, giving public recognition to its status; and under this charter it still functions, in republican Dublin, as the Royal Irish Academy.

The date of the Academy's foundation is significant. It was a time when the sense of achievement that accompanied the 'Constitution of 1782' was still alive and when national pride was strong among the Anglo-Irish. But it was also a time when public opinion was deeply, even bitterly, divided over parliamentary reform and the admission of Roman Catholics to political power. And yet, despite these political divisions, in which its own members were no less involved than other citizens, the Academy succeeded in establishing itself as a place from which such controversies were excluded, a place where men of different parties and different faiths could meet together, on friendly and equal terms, in pursuit of their scholarly interests. It was, from the beginning, a national body, fostering especially the study of Irish history and antiquities, but without any of the rancour of nationalism. It expressed, in corporate form, much of what was best in Anglo-Irish society; and the tradition it established was maintained, in the very different circumstances of succeeding generations, almost to the present day.

The Dublin Society and the Royal Irish Academy were inspired, though in different ways, by a sense of national responsibility and national identity. The literary life of the Anglo-Irish at the same period shows no such national spirit. Even while they were insisting most strongly on the constitutional rights of Ireland as a distinct kingdom it did not occur to them to impose any such distinction in the world of literature: here, Ireland and England shared a common heritage, where national boundaries had no place. Ireland and England formed, in fact, a single literary world, of which London was the natural capital; and critical judgements promulgated there were equally current on both sides of the Irish Sea. People with a taste for what the eighteenth century called 'polite literature', whether they lived in Ireland or England, read the same books, admired the same authors and saw the same plays in their theatres. It is hardly surprising, then, that the Irish writer of the period, whether he aimed at reputation or at profit, should have his eyes fixed on London. It was on the judgement of the London critics that fame depended; it was in London that the best chance of fortune lay; and, if fame and fortune failed, it was only in London that the struggling author could hope to hold starvation at bay by the labour of his pen. Even those Irish authors who, from choice or necessity, resided in their native land felt the attractive power of London and commonly preferred to publish their works there rather than in Dublin.

These circumstances influenced, one might almost say determined, the character of Irish writing during the period. Irish authors inherited the common tradition of English literature. As poets, playwrights, essayists, novelists, they followed the same models as their fellow-authors of English birth, felt themselves to belong to the same community and addressed themselves to the same public. Their writings show no common stamp of a distinctively national character. Eighteenth-century Irish architecture, metalwork, glassware and book-bindings have a character of their own; and an expert can recognize them as Irish, even without any external evidence of their origin. With literature, the case is quite different. Here we find no common style, no coherent development of form and technique, no succession of leadership from one generation to another. In short, though there was a great deal of literary interest and literary activity among the Anglo-Irish of the eighteenth century, there did not emerge any body of work that could properly be called an Anglo-Irish literature.

This does not mean, of course, that the Irish-born writers of the period owed nothing to the background from which they came. Even though the literary public of Ireland was an extension of that of England and looked to London for guidance, it could not escape the force of geographical circumstances. For most Irishmen of literary taste, London itself was out of reach; and they maintained their contact with the great world through Dublin, which was the cultural as well as the political capital of the kingdom. Dublin, it is true, could offer little to the author who hoped to make his way in the world by his writings; but it none the less had an active literary life, which extended its influence to every part of the country. The people who maintained this activity—minor gentry, clergy and lawyers, for the most part—had no claim to greatness; their works, even their names, are now hardly remembered. But, even so, they had a part to play. Literary genius rarely springs from a bare ground. It flourishes best when it is rooted in a living tradition and when its early growth has the encouragement of familiar example. This succession of minor writers, forgotten, or half-forgotten today, kept alive the tradition that produced Jonathan Swift and George Berkeley, Edmund Burke, Oliver Goldsmith and Richard Brinsley Sheridan—a quintet of genius that could hardly be matched, and certainly not surpassed, among the English-born writers of the period.

Though the writings of these five authors form part of the general corpus of English literature, the men themselves were products of the Anglo-Irish community. All five came from that middle class on which so much of the Anglo-Irish achievement rested. Swift and Burke were the sons of lawyers; Goldsmith and Sheridan belonged, though Sheridan at one remove, to clerical families with connections among the minor gentry; Berkeley's father was a revenue official who also had some landed interest, though more probably as a tenant than as a proprietor. But their families, though similar in social status, differed considerably in the length of their association with Ireland. Sheridan belonged to an anglicized branch of an ancient Gaelic sept, while Swift had been born only a few years after his parents had left England and established themselves in Dublin; and the three others represented various intervening layers of settlement. Thus they spanned between them almost the whole range of Anglo-Irish origins.

The cultural environment in which they grew to maturity was essentially Anglo-Irish. So far as Sheridan was concerned, this was a matter of family influence rather than of formal education; after a brief period in a Dublin school he was sent to Harrow at the age of eleven and remained there for six years. But his development as a writer owed much more to his parents than to his teachers; and his parents were typical representatives of the Anglo-Irish literary tradition. His father, a son of the Thomas Sheridan who had been the friend and correspondent of Swift, had taken a leading part in the theatrical life of Dublin before settling in England as a teacher of elocution and self-styled 'orthoepist'. His mother, who came from a Dublin clerical family with a taste for literature, was a well-known novelist and the author of a very successful comedy. It is hardly surprising that Sheridan, brought up in such a household, should have turned to literature before he was out of his teens. None of the others had the same kind of family example to encourage or guide them; but they, unlike Sheridan, received the whole of their education in Ireland and all four were graduates of Trinity College, Dublin. Their outlook, no less than his, was moulded by the cultural tradition of the Anglo-Irish.

But this tradition did not express itself in any distinct literary form. There is no characteristic style of writing or mode of treating a theme that one can confidently label as peculiarly 'Anglo-Irish'; and where the great Anglo-Irish writers of the eighteenth century reveal the influence of their background it is in an essentially individual way. How far this influence pervades their work and how much it contributed to their achievement is a matter on which literary critics disagree. But, whatever the outcome of the argument may be, the authors themselves are unmistakably and characteristically Anglo-Irish. Their work is not only part of the heritage of the English-speaking world; it is also a living memorial of the eighteenth-century Kingdom of Ireland.

(5)

Eighteenth-century Ireland was a Protestant kingdom, governed under a Protestant constitution; and the whole Protestant population, from the members of parliament at College Green to the linen weavers of County Armagh, was convinced of its right to a position of ascendancy in Ireland. Not until the 1790s was this claim openly challenged; but the character of the challenge when it came, and its significance for the future, were strongly influenced by the social conditions that had prevailed throughout the century.

In Ireland, as elsewhere in contemporary Europe, the wealth created by the labour of the many was largely concentrated in the hands of a few; and the contrast between rich and poor was sharply marked. In some countries the resentment provoked by gross inequality was softened by the sense of community between different classes; but over most of Ireland such a sense of community was rarely to be found. The landlords and their tenants were separated by more than a divergence of economic interests. Traditional memories of conquest and confiscation remained alive among the peasantry and were strengthened by religious distinctions. The easier relationship between landlord and tenant that prevailed in most parts of Ulster had its basis in their common Protestantism as well as in the more prosperous condition of the province. Even in Ulster the grievances of the tenants gave rise to occasional disorder; but such outbreaks were few and short-lived; and they left no lasting scar. Elsewhere the situation was different; and from the middle of the century onwards agrarian unrest was endemic over much of Munster and in parts of Leinster. Bands of 'Whiteboys' (as they were commonly called) scoured the countryside by night, houghing cattle, destroying property, attacking and torturing those who had incurred their displeasure. The origin of this campaign of terrorism may be traced to the action of certain landlords who had evicted tenants in order to amalgamate their holdings into large grazing-farms, which they found more profitable. But the campaign, once begun, continued and spread; the tenants had found a method of asserting themselves and they were ready to employ it wherever there was an advantage to be gained or an injury to be avenged. Such a challenge to the rights of property terrified the landlords, especially as the ordinary forces of the law seemed incapable of meeting it; and parliament passed a series of repressive measures, so severe that they seemed, in Arthur Young's view, to be 'calculated for the meridian of Barbary'. But even such rigorous action was insufficient to restore order. It is very doubtful if, once the habit of violence had established itself, a policy of conciliation and concession would have been any more successful; but it was a policy that the landlords never entertained. They met force with force and in some areas they managed to restore their authority, at least for a time; but they were unable to establish a general and lasting peace and the measures they employed increased the resentment of the tenantry.

Though it was widely asserted at the time that the Whiteboy movement was politically inspired and was fomented by French agents, there is no convincing evidence to support this assertion. The Whiteboys were no more than what they professed to be—an association of tenants determined to gain what they regarded as their rights by force, since they could not gain them by law. But in the circumstances of later eighteenth-century Ireland agrarian unrest could easily be turned into a political channel; and this is what happened in the 1790s, when the United Irishmen tried to disseminate the principles of the French Revolution through the countryside. Except in the north, where the Presbyterian link with America had prepared the way for the reception of political ideas, they made most headway in areas where agrarian agitation was widespread; and a connection was formed between the nationalist demand for freedom from English rule and the tenants' demand for redress of their grievances. This connection, at first very vague, became clearly and firmly established in the nineteenth century and exercised a powerful influence on the character of the nationalist movement. Even after the whole landlord system had been swept away and former tenants had been put in full possession of their lands, the spirit of agrarian agitation, of a conflict between oppressed and oppressor, remained alive. Irish nationalism, in its more violent expression, has commonly displayed the blind hatred, brutal cruelty and wanton destructiveness that are characteristic of a servile war.

The tumultuous events of the 1790s have made such a strong impression on later generations that the real achievements of the eighteenth century have often been forgotten or misrepresented. The Ireland of the Protestant ascendancy was more prosperous and more liberal than has commonly been recognized; and its constitution provided for the possibility, at least, of a gradual and peaceful broadening of the basis of authority. But all was changed by the impact of the French Revolution; and the earlier period, seen through the blood-stained mist of the insurrection of 1798 and its aftermath, appears remote and artificial. The legacy of hatred and violence still remains; and while it continues to dominate the minds of men few will do justice to the Irish Nation of Swift and Grattan.

V

'*An English Garrison*'

(1)

If a stranger who had been in Ireland during the height of the controversy over the union had returned some five or six years later he might well have found himself wondering what all the fuss had been about. The viceroy still held court in Dublin, and the Castle was still the headquarters of an Irish administration. The country as a whole, even if it showed little sign of the new prosperity promised by Pitt and Castlereagh, was at least not obviously worse off than it had been. The whole union controversy seemed to be dead and buried. And if the visitor had asked after the Patriot leaders whose fiery eloquence had thundered in parliament and been spread over the country in pamphlets and newspapers he would have found that they had laid aside their rage, now that the occasion for it was over, and were peacefully pursuing their careers, either at home or in England.

John Foster, the Speaker of the House of Commons, had crowned his stalwart opposition to union by refusing to surrender the mace, the symbol of his office, 'until the body that had entrusted it to his keeping demanded it'. But this was an empty gesture: Foster transferred himself to Westminster, and in 1804 he accepted office under Pitt, the very minister responsible for the union. William Plunket, after Grattan the most effective of the anti-union debaters, had promised a resistance that was to endure even after his death:

> For my own part, I will resist it [union] to the last gasp of my existence and with the last drop of my blood, and when I feel the hour of my dissolution approaching I will, like the father of Hannibal, take my children to the altar and swear them to hostility against the invaders of their country's freedom.

But in 1803 Plunket took office as solicitor-general for Ireland; and when, in 1805, he was appointed attorney-general, his successor was Charles Kendal Bushe, the 'incorruptible', who had refused to accept the Mastership of the Rolls in exchange for a vote in favour of the union. In the same year, Grattan himself, the very incarnation of Irish parliamentary independence, took his seat at Westminster, at first for an English constituency; and, though he devoted himself mainly to Irish affairs, and above all to the cause of Catholic Emancipation, he neither raised the question of the union nor even attempted to form a distinctively Irish party. It might seem as if the whole furious and dramatic struggle over the union had been no more than a sham fight, after which victors and vanquished could settle down together and resume the ordinary business of life.

But this is to over-simplify the situation. Opposition to the union, though undoubtedly mingled with selfish and sectional interests, had been genuine and deep-felt. The anti-unionists, however narrow their outlook, were proud of being Irishmen, proud of their country's position as a nation among the nations of Europe, and they were unwilling to barter it for any advantage that might be offered. But when the battle had been fought and lost at College Green they saw no means of continuing the struggle. Acquiescence seemed the only course open to them; and they adjusted themselves to the new conditions more quickly and with less difficulty than might have been expected. The great Irish political families had, after all, the same kind of background and the same kind of interests as their counterparts in Britain. There is nothing surprising in the fact that George Ponsonby, who had led the Whig opposition at College Green, should subsequently lead the Whig opposition at Westminster, nor even in the fact that he should signalize his new position by transferring from an Irish to an English constituency. For men of his class, the parliamentary union, whether they had opposed or supported it, opened the way to a more important sphere of action: if they had lost their exclusive position in the government of a kingdom, they had gained a share in the government of an empire.

So far as the average country gentleman was concerned, the changes brought about by the union were not, in the short run, of much obvious significance. The reduction in the number of Irish M.P.s had, it is true, cut down his chance of a seat in parliament; but, otherwise, things went on much as before. His chief political concern had always been to maintain the strength of his influence in county elections and to get his full share of government patronage; and the means of attaining these ends remained unchanged. For the rest, his political creed was simple: the protection of property and the maintenance of order. However deeply he had drunk damnation to Pitt, Castlereagh and the unionists in 1800, he soon found himself happy enough with the new state of affairs. In any case, he had no inclination to stand by a hopeless cause at the certain cost of excluding himself from government favour and the probable risk of encouraging popular discontent. From this, it was not a far step to accepting the union as the best guarantee of his own position.

It is, naturally enough, the attitude of the landed classes, who dominated parliamentary life, that most readily attracts attention; but the rank and file of the Anglo-Irish community were equally concerned. They, too, had been deeply divided over the union, though it is impossible to say with confidence on which side of the division majority opinion lay. The evidence would suggest, however, that the supporters of union were rarely inspired by much enthusiasm, while its opponents were active, well-organized, and loud in their professions of patriotic zeal. But, once the union came into force, all this opposition speedily died away. There was no machinery to keep it in being, nor any prospect that defeat could be reversed. Even in Dublin, though tradesmen might grumble about loss of business, now that parliament no longer met in the city and the nobility were closing up their town houses, union had to be accepted as a fact that men must learn to live with. And it soon became clear that the change was not so disastrous as it might have been. Though the legislature had been removed to Westminster, Ireland retained its own distinct executive. 'The Castle' was still the centre of authority; and the spirit of Castle administration was almost unchanged. Protestant fears, particularly strong among the Orange Societies, that union would immediately be followed by concessions to the Roman Catholics, proved unfounded. Ireland had lost its status as a distinct kingdom; but it was still to be governed by Protestants and under a Protestant constitution. It was not long before Irish Protestants in general, whatever side they had taken in the great struggle of 1799 and 1800, began to feel that they were safer in a United Kingdom with a large Protestant majority than they could ever be as a small minority in a self-governing Ireland.

If the parliamentary union had worked out as those who planned it had hoped, if Ireland had become merged with Great Britain as fully and peaceably as Scotland had been merged with England, then the acquiescence of the Anglo-Irish in the new state of affairs would call for no special comment. But Ireland was a deeply divided country. It was hardly possible to envisage a settlement that would satisfy one part of the population without alienating the other; and the very circumstances that made union so speedily acceptable to the Protestants made it almost intolerable to the Roman Catholics. The longstanding conflict between the two, changed in form but not in substance, remained the dominant factor in Irish political life.

The change in the form of the conflict was to prove of decisive importance for the Anglo-Irish. By accepting the parliamentary union they had surrendered completely control of their destiny. They could no longer defend their own interests in their own way, but must rely directly and solely upon the government in London. It is true, of course, that even before 1800 the Irish executive had been controlled from England; but it had never been able to ignore the Irish parliament; and, on questions of law and order, parliament commonly had its way. Besides this, there were military forces available that were distinctively Irish. Claims made by the anti-unionists that the rebellion of 1798 had been broken by the militia and yeomanry before reinforcements arrived from England, though no doubt exaggerated, were not without substance. But now, if a similar crisis arose, immediate responsibility for every decision would rest with the British cabinet, where the interests of Protestant Ireland would not be the only, or even the main, consideration. It was not very likely, perhaps, that an insurrection on the scale of 1798 would recur; but the possibility of an outbreak of some sort could never be ignored; and over much of the country agrarian disorder was endemic. Behind all lay the resentment of the Catholic population at the survival of Protestant hegemony and a determination that, by some means or other, it should be destroyed; while the Protestants, who believed that their position, their property, and even their lives were in constant jeopardy, were fearful lest the government, in the hope of conciliating Catholic opinion, would deliver them over to their enemies. And yet, whatever their fears and suspicions about government policy, the Protestants had no alternative but to support the union. No longer able to defend themselves, they must accept the defence afforded by Britain, on whatever terms it was offered.

As the century progressed, and the smouldering resentment of the Roman Catholics began to express itself in party organization, the line of political division in Ireland became even more explicit: Roman Catholics demanded the re-establishment of an Irish parliament; Protestants stood for the maintenance of the union. Though there were exceptions on both sides, they were too few to affect the general picture; and on the great issue of relations between Ireland and Britain Catholics and Protestants stood face to face in irreconcilable opposition. In these circumstances it is hardly surprising that Irish Protestants came to be seen by their opponents as the allies and agents of government, as the means whereby an alien power held down an oppressed and discontented people—in short, as an 'English Garrison' in a conquered country.

It was a description that fitted the situation of the Protestants rather than their outlook. Like Burke in the previous century they believed that Ireland could prosper only as a part of the Empire, and in subjection to the imperial power of Britain; and, again like Burke, they could not see why this belief should weaken their claim to be Irish. This commitment to the imperial connection, though one need not doubt its honesty, suited their own interests, for they soon came to believe that their position in Ireland depended upon the maintenance of the union. Thus they were forced into defending a political system that the great mass of their fellow-countrymen resented; and they themselves often emphasized the internal division of the country by insisting on their own 'loyalty', which they contrasted with the 'disloyalty' that they attributed to the Catholic population in general. British governments, desperately anxious to secure peace in Ireland, whether by coercion or conciliation or by a judicious mixture of the two, could not afford to accept this simple contrast; and they often followed policies that alarmed the Protestant minority. But the Protestants, even when they were most discontented with the practical effects of the union, could see no alternative to supporting it: however distasteful government by a British parliament might be, government by an Irish parliament would be infinitely worse. Throughout the whole period of the union the Protestants were the only element in the population that maintained, through thick and thin, that Ireland was and must remain an integral part of the United Kingdom.

But if the Irish Protestants were in truth a garrison, they were a garrison in peculiar and difficult circumstances. Though almost perpetually under siege, they had neither means nor authority to organize their own defence. They must work always under orders from a remote headquarters, where strategy and tactics were liable to frequent fluctuations and where the enemy could often exercise as much influence as the garrison itself. They had no power to come to terms on their own behalf; but they lived in constant fear that terms would be arranged behind their backs; that a vital outwork might suddenly be surrendered; and even that, sooner or later, the whole fortress would be abandoned and they themselves left to their fate.

(2)

Those who spoke of the Anglo-Irish as an 'English garrison' commonly thought of them as no more than a small and privileged landlord class. But after the union, as before, the Anglo-Irish community extended over the whole economic and social range; and many of its most distinguished members came from the middle and lower ranks. Yet this emphasis on the position of the landlords is understandable. In the course of the nineteenth century their relationship with the main body of the Anglo-Irish underwent a change: they became more important as spokesmen and champions of the Anglo-Irish position; and yet, at the same time, they became more isolated; and both circumstances exposed them to attack. This development was, in part, a product of the union; but it owed even more to constitutional changes later in the century.

Before the union, the Irish parliament, though dominated by the landlords, had not been able to ignore completely the trend of public opinion among the Protestant population in general; and from the 1760s onward that opinion had been able to exercise a strong influence on the attitude of the House of Commons. In the nineteenth century the situation was quite different. Irish M.P.s at Westminster quickly lost any sense of a corporate national responsibility; and, apart from this, mere distance weakened the impact of popular opinion at home on their attitudes and actions.* But constitutional changes did even more to reduce the rank and file of the Protestant population to political impotence. In 1829 Catholic Emancipation opened parliament to Roman Catholics; and the Reform Act of 1832 increased their voting strength in the boroughs. Together, these measures undermined, and almost destroyed, the basis on which the ascendancy of the Anglo-Irish had rested since the seventeenth century. The political influence of property declined, while that of numbers rose; and since Catholic voters were now free to elect Catholic members, their numerical superiority would enable them to dominate the parliamentary representation of Ireland. The act of 1832 did not itself go far enough to bring about such a drastic change in the balance of power; but the process then begun was completed by later extensions of the franchise; and before the end of the century Roman Catholic electors returned more than eighty per cent of the Irish M.P.s.

Throughout most of the country, then, the Protestant population almost ceased to count in parliamentary politics. In the three southern provinces there were some hundreds of thousands of Protestants—labourers, farmers, shopkeepers, merchants, lawyers and other professional

* Cf. the remark of Mrs Howden in Scott's *Heart of Midlothian*: 'When we had a king, and a chancellor, and parliament-men o' our ain, we could aye peeble them wi' stanes when they werena gude bairns—But naebody's nails can reach the length o' Lunnon.'

men; but only here and there were they numerous enough to carry any weight in elections. Their eighteenth-century ancestors had manned the ranks of the Volunteers, had celebrated Grattan's victory in 1782, had signed addresses for or against the union—had had, in fact, reason to feel that they could take some part, however obscure, in the public life of the kingdom. But by the middle of the nineteenth century all this had been changed; and the Protestants of the south and west now found that neither their support nor their opposition could alter the balance of political power and that no government was likely to be influenced by any opinion they might express.

The situation was quite different in Ulster, where the Protestants formed a majority, though not a very large majority, of the total population and here, even after Emancipation and parliamentary reform, they could still elect a substantial body of M.P.s. But more than half the Ulster Protestants were Presbyterians of Scottish descent, who regarded the established church with some suspicion and whose social and cultural links were with Scotland rather than England. Partly because of their closely knit ecclesiastical organization, partly because they formed a large proportion of the wealthy middle class, the influence of the Presbyterians was even greater than their numbers would suggest; and it coloured the outlook of Ulster Protestants in general. They had not yet begun to substitute a local for an Irish loyalty; but they were very conscious of the distinctive character of their province and increasingly inclined to look down on the rest of the country. Nineteenth-century Ulster, in fact, can hardly be regarded as Anglo-Irish territory. Among members of the established church, who included almost all the landlords, there was a sense of community with their fellow-churchmen in the south and west; but among most of them this did not prove strong enough to resist the pressure for political separation that later became so powerful. If we are to understand the position and outlook of the Anglo-Irish in the nineteenth and twentieth centuries we must look away from Ulster and concentrate our attention on the Protestant minority in Leinster, Munster and Connaught.

In these three provinces the Protestants were too few and too scattered to acquire weight in parliament; and the reform of the municipal corporations in 1840 broke their longstanding monopoly of power in the cities and boroughs. It seemed as if Lord John George Beresford's prophecy of 1829 was coming true and that the effect of government policy would be to 'transfer from Protestants to Roman Catholics the ascendancy of Ireland'. It was this state of affairs that gave a new importance to the fact that the greater part of the land remained in Protestant ownership: the landlords could still hope that their wealth and position would give them some voice in public affairs. It was true that their power to control their tenants' votes in parliamentary election had now almost gone; and what was left of their borough interest after the Reform Act of 1832 was destroyed by later legislation. But county administration remained in their hands until the establishment of elective councils in 1898. And they still had some means, direct and indirect, of influencing government policy. Many of them sat in the House of Lords, either in their own right or as Irish representative peers; and others represented English constituencies in the House of Commons. Besides this, their social position gave them easy access to those who exercised power, whether in London or in Dublin; and though it is impossible to assess the nature or the extent of the influence they could exert in this way, they had at least an opportunity of putting their case forward. Even if they accomplished nothing else, they obliged the government to remember that there was a 'Protestant interest' in the south and west of Ireland, a fact that some British politicians, especially in the later part of the century, would have been glad to forget.

In a sense, then, the landlords may be regarded as spokesmen for the whole body of the Anglo-Irish; and they were, at the time, the only people who could have filled that rôle. But they did not act in any representative capacity; they did not seek to reflect Protestant opinion in general; and their policy, in so far as they had one, was essentially a landlord policy. Later on, in the last decades of the union, when the imminent threat of Home Rule brought Protestants of all classes together in organized self-defence, the landlords were accepted as natural leaders, resting on the support of the whole Protestant population; but for the greater part of the nineteenth century they stood in apparent isolation, an easy target for attack.

Throughout the whole period of the parliamentary union the character and conduct of the Irish landlords was a matter of bitter controversy. The propaganda of their critics was so effective that it converted British public opinion; and historians have generally been inclined to accept it almost at its face value. Only in recent years has a patient sifting of evidence begun to call in question allegations that have long been regarded almost as self-evident truths. In fact, rents were rarely excessive; and they rose much more slowly than the price of agricultural produce, so that most of the increased income went to the tenants, not to the landlords. Evictions, even for non-payment of rent, were far less frequent than the traditional view asserts; and arbitrary or capricious use of the power of eviction was very unusual indeed. Irish landlords were not good managers; they were often hampered by debt accumulated through extravagance; they did little to improve their estates. But they were not the cruel and grasping tyrants, wringing the last penny of rent from a starving and terrified tenantry, that their enemies have made them appear.

The tenants had, of course, some good grounds for discontent. The landlord's power of eviction, even if he seldom used it, gave him a much greater degree of authority than that of an employer over his workmen: a dismissed employee might get another job; a tenant who lost his land was almost helpless. A rise in rent, even if justified by a rise in the price of produce, had the same effect as a lowering of wages and aroused the same kind of resentment. But there were other parts of the British Isles where tenants were liable to eviction and where rents rose with the price of agricultural produce, and yet there was no agrarian violence nor any general outcry against landlords. Even in north-western Scotland, where rural conditions resembled those in parts of Ireland and where relations between landlord and tenant were sometimes strained to breaking-point, there was no widespread and sustained attack on the whole landlord system, such as occurred in Ireland.

The truth is that what distinguished the Irish tenants was not so much their condition as their attitude. They had inherited from the eighteenth century a tradition of agrarian violence, so that physical attack upon anyone whom they regarded as an enemy seemed to them the most natural line of action. From a more remote past they had inherited a belief that the landlords were alien usurpers, conquerors who had stolen their estates from the rightful owners and now held them by force. In an almost static rural society, where the same families might occupy the same farms generation after generation, there was a long folk memory. The names of former proprietors were kept alive; and those who had replaced them, marked off by a different religious faith, were still regarded as strangers after a lapse of more than two centuries. This feeling was not, of course, universal. Loyalty to the family in possession was often expressed and, no doubt, sometimes genuine. Miss Edgeworth's correspondence reveals the affection with which the family was regarded by the tenantry on their estate in County Longford; and there is much other evidence to the same effect. But where tenant and landlord were in conflict old memories had a potent influence; and behind the tenant's demand for a reduction in the rent, or his protest against an increase, there often lay a conviction that he was under no moral obligation to pay any rent at all to 'the Saxon'.

The belief that the landlords were not only oppressive but alien goes back a long way; but it was the Great Famine that fixed it unshakeably, not only in the mind of the Catholic tenantry, but in the mind of the Catholic population at large: the British government had, they believed, been responsible for the disaster, but the conduct of the landlords had made it even more terrible. James Anthony Froude, who visited the west of Ireland both on the eve of the Famine and after the worst of the suffering was over, noted a change in attitude. In 1845 he found 'that there was no visible ill-feeling between the serfs and their masters. The Orange lord was still the master whom they loved in their way, especially when he was out at elbows like themselves.' But in 1848 it was different: 'There is the most genuine hatred of the Irish landlords everywhere through the country that I can remember to have heard expressed of person or thing.' Froude was sometimes inclined to picturesque exaggeration; and his comments cannot be taken at their face value. But there can be no doubt at all that the Famine brought a new degree of bitterness into relations between landlord and tenant and encouraged the popular belief that the landlords were the enemies of Ireland. Some landlords had, in fact, taken advantage of the Famine to clear their overcrowded estates by evicting the poorer tenants. Others had devoted themselves and their whole resources to the work of relief. All had suffered economic loss; and some had been brought to bankruptcy. But public opinion made few distinctions or allowances; and the landlord class as a whole fell under a general condemnation.

In this more hostile atmosphere the campaign against the landlords took on a new character. Agrarian disorder, fomented by secret societies, still continued, though it was probably less serious than contemporary reports would suggest. But, side by side with this, there grew up an open political movement, designed to work through parliament for a radical change in the law relating to land-tenure. The movement achieved little on its own; but in the 1870s its policy was taken over by the newly formed Home Rule party. From this time onwards, the demand for self-government was identified with an unremitting attack on the status and power of the landlords. Home Rule politicians constantly encouraged and magnified the grievances of the tenants; and the total destruction of the landlord system came to be regarded as an essential step in the process of making Ireland 'a nation once again'. In this struggle, the actual character of the system became almost irrelevant, except in so far as its abuses might provide material for propaganda. The real issue was no longer social or economic, but political; and the real object was to wrest property, and the influence that went with it, out of the hands of men who were regarded as enemies of the nation.

This generally hostile popular opinion made it impossible for an Irish landlord to play the same sort of rôle in the local community as might be played by a landlord in England. Indeed, the two countries were so utterly different both in actual conditions and in historical backgrounds, that no fair comparison can be made. A good many Irish landlords—more than is commonly recognized—did, in fact, try to improve the lot of their tenants and promote the general welfare of their neighbourhoods. But they generally found it an uphill task, in which only a determined man was likely to persevere for long. One such man was John Hamilton, of St. Ernan's, in County Donegal, one of the poorest parts of Ulster, where the population was predominantly Roman Catholic and where relations between landlord and tenant were, in general, less harmonious than they were in the province as a whole. Hamilton had thus to face the same sort of social and economic difficulties as landlords in the three southern provinces; and his experience is worth examining in some detail. He had succeeded, as a minor, to a large but impoverished estate, of which he took possession on attaining his majority in 1821. He devoted the next sixty years of his life to improving the condition of his tenants. Instead of working through an agent he managed everything himself. He moved freely among the tenants, giving advice and listening to their complaints; he visited their homes and knew the particular circumstances of every family on the estate. He built houses, drained land, constructed roads, established and maintained schools. To begin with, at least, he found the result of his efforts disappointing: many of those for whom he had done most remained, as before, shiftless, ragged and dirty. But he refused to give up. Year after year he continued his help and his exhortations; the standard of farming and of cleanliness gradually improved; and even the local parish priest, a noted critic of landlordism in general, bore public witness to his kindness and his popularity. Hamilton may have found it easier to win the confidence of his tenants because he held aloof from party politics, though he did issue warnings, from time to time, about the folly of being misled by political or agrarian agitators. But he was a strong, if not strictly orthodox, Protestant; and, while not seeking controversy, he lost no opportunity of proclaiming his religious views. Religion was, indeed, the dominant influence in his life and inspired the sense of duty that guided him in the management of his estate. His conviction that only when others came under the same influence would society be happy made him suspicious of attempts to improve the state of affairs by legislation. In an address to his tenants on Gladstone's land act of 1870, he warned them: 'Even if the law could make all landlords do right, it would be little use, unless it could make all *tenants* wise, prudent, industrious and good.'

Hamilton attained a considerable measure of success; but it was attained only by patient and unremitting devotion to duty, inspired and informed by strong religious conviction. And, in the end, the success was only partial. In his last address to his tenants, issued after sixty years of life among them, one can detect a note of disappointment behind the friendly style; and his statement that he now favours the winding up of the whole landlord system by a policy of land purchase reads almost like a confession of defeat.

Hamilton was certainly not typical; indeed, men of his stamp are rare in any community. But it is the very fact that he was untypical that makes his experience instructive. Here was a landlord of determined character, impelled by a strong sense of duty arising from religious conviction; in the course of a long life he won the affection of his tenants and the approval even of those who were opposed to landlordism in general; and yet, in the end, he was forced to the conclusion that there was no place for landlords in the social and economic life of Ireland. And this conclusion did not arise from any doubts about his own policy, but from a slow and reluctant acceptance of the fact that the tenants did not want any landlords at all. If Hamilton—whom even that hammer of the Irish landlords, Mr. Gladstone, felt himself obliged to praise—had to make this confession, it seems fair to conclude that the fate of the landlords was inescapable. Their own character and conduct may have hastened their fall, and certainly embittered the struggle that preceded it. But, once the voting power of the Roman Catholic majority had been organized in the cause of Home Rule, the landlords, who were the outstanding representatives of Protestant ascendancy and the leading supporters of the parliamentary union, could not survive indefinitely.

In their own day, the Irish landlords never succeeded in arousing much sympathy; and it is only recently that historians have begun seriously to question the justice of the charges usually levelled against them. They were, in fact, the victims of circumstance, rather than of any peculiar degree of folly or vice on their own part. To the Catholic majority, they were both a relic and a symbol of conquest, confiscation and tyranny. By the British government they came to be regarded as the principal barrier to a solution of the perennial 'Irish Question'. Caught between these two forces, they could do nothing but submit on the best terms they could get. It is rarely possible, in the examination of any historical development, to assess separately the importance of the various factors that have contributed to bring it about; but, in considering the fall of the Irish landlords, one may safely say that mismanagement of their estates would have counted less heavily against them if they had shown themselves more sympathetic to the rising cause of Catholic nationalism.

(3)

Though the Anglo-Irish accepted the union so readily when once it was established, and became its most stalwart supporters, they did not cease to think of themselves as Irishmen. Ireland was still their country, indissolubly linked with England and Scotland, but yet distinct from either; and they cherished the surviving symbols of its former status. Their interest in Irish history and Irish antiquities, which had developed in the eighteenth century, did not die away when Ireland ceased to be an independent kingdom; indeed, it became stronger, more widespread and more fruitful. But their sense of being Irish, though still deeply felt, had lost all political content. They were citizens of the United Kingdom; and it was to the larger entity that their allegiance was now due. Their former zeal for the national rights of Ireland seemed to have burned itself out. Even the Protestants of Ulster, the cradle of the United Irish movement, were soon to be found among the foremost defenders of the union with Britain.

It is tempting to sum up the situation by saying that after the union Irish Protestants deserted the nationalist cause. But this is only part of the truth. It is no less important to remember that the cause deserted them, for the kind of nationalism in which they had been bred was now giving way to a movement of a very different character. The course of this development had already been foreshadowed in 1798. The Protestant leaders who prepared the way for rebellion had been bred in the Volunteer tradition, revivified and given a new direction by the example of Revolutionary France; but this tradition meant nothing to the Catholic peasantry of Wexford, who bore the main brunt of the fighting. Fanatical alike in their courage and in their ferocity, they were moved by an ancient sense of oppression and deprivation and sustained by religious fervour. The spirit in which they fought was to exercise, from that time onwards, a continuing influence on Irish nationalism, even when it expressed itself in constitutional form; and the religious commitment that contributed so much to their sense of solidarity remained, through all subsequent changes, an outstanding characteristic of the main stream of Irish nationalism.

It is easy to understand why this should have been so. The Roman Catholic church was the one public institution in which the great bulk of the people could see embodied their sense of a corporate national existence. During the period of the penal laws, when the church was struggling to maintain its institutional framework, the clergy had been cautious and unobtrusive. But even before the end of the eighteenth century signs of a change were evident; and after the union the bishops gradually came to be regarded as national spokesmen, on secular as well as on religious matters. This development was hastened by the manner in which O'Connell conducted his Emancipation campaign in the later 1820s. He roused the Roman Catholics to united popular effort under the leadership of the parochial clergy; and he gave them a sense of cohesion and confidence such as they had never known before. His success in achieving Emancipation was hailed as a national victory; and this alliance of Church and People laid down the lines along which nationalism was to advance.

The strength of this alliance was noted by Alexis de Tocqueville during his visit to Ireland in 1835. Over and over again he was struck by the close ties of political sympathy between the clergy and their people. The bishops seemed to him 'as much the leaders of a party as the representatives of the church'; and he detected in what they said about the state of Ireland 'an air of exaltation' and 'a note of triumph', as over a victory already won or fast approaching. He found the Protestants equally insistent on the identity between religion and politics. One of them, a barrister, summed up the situation as he saw it: 'For the Irish [meaning, of course, the Roman Catholics] religion is not only a question of faith; it is also a question of patriotism.' Less than a decade later, O'Connell's newspaper, the *Pilot*, was even more explicit, asserting plainly that the 'positive and unmistakable' mark of distinction between Irish and English was 'the distinction created by religion'. O'Connell himself might not have subscribed to this view; but in making himself the champion of the Catholic cause he had, even if unwillingly, identified that cause with the cause of Ireland; and it was beyond his power to separate the two. A nationalism so closely linked with the Roman Catholic church could hardly appeal to the Anglo-Irish. If their own concept of 'the Irish nation' had been narrowly based, it had been

G   97

succeeded by a concept that appeared, in practice, almost equally exclusive.

It could, of course, be argued that this exclusiveness was the fault of the Anglo-Irish themselves. By accepting the union they had abandoned their duty to defend the national rights of Ireland and they could not complain if that duty were now assumed by others. But a self-conscious minority is rarely willing to surrender its identity; and the Anglo-Irish believed that if the union were dissolved their distinctive traditions and characteristics would be crushed out of existence by the weight of the Catholic majority. Indeed, the very vigour and enthusiasm with which that majority pressed its demand for the re-establishment of an Irish parliament served to strengthen their fears of what would happen if power should ever pass into Catholic hands. Yet, in every generation, there were some among them to whom these fears seemed irrelevant, who were so strongly convinced of Ireland's right to govern itself that every other issue fell into the background. Such men made an important contribution to the nationalist movement; but it can hardly be said that they modified its essentially Catholic character.

This nationalist element among the Anglo-Irish did not make any great impression on the public until the 1840s, when O'Connell launched a massive campaign for the repeal of the act of union. He had announced this policy a good deal earlier; but it was only now that he threw the whole of his immense energy behind it. He set up a Repeal Association to raise funds and organize meetings, at which his violent denunciations of the government and his demands for Repeal were applauded by hundreds of thousands of enthusiastic supporters. His purpose was to demonstrate that popular opinion was irresistibly behind him. But he realized that his case would appear much stronger if he could show that his movement was not merely a sectarian one; and so, though he depended heavily on the Roman Catholic clergy, without whom his organization could hardly have functioned effectively, he sought eagerly for Protestant support. He sought to little purpose: no substantial body of Protestants rallied to the cause of Repeal; and the main organs of Protestant opinion were everywhere against it. But among the Protestants who did join the Association there were some who played a prominent part in its affairs, even though their presence did nothing to alter its general character. The pattern thus set survived throughout the period of the union: the nationalist movement expressed the will of the Catholic majority, but it was always able to draw spokesmen and leaders from the ranks of the Protestant minority.

The small band of Protestants who supported O'Connell in the 1840s included several whose names are still remembered; and two of these, William Smith O'Brien and Thomas Davis, may fairly be taken as representing the kind of contribution that the Anglo-Irish made to the nationalist cause that most of them utterly rejected. Smith O'Brien, a well-to-do landlord of ancient Gaelic stock, entered parliament in April 1828 as a follower of Sir Robert Peel. Within a few months, he had declared his support for Catholic Emancipation; and in succeeding years he concentrated his parliamentary activity on issues affecting Ireland. But he retained for a long time his faith in the principle of union; and it was not until 1843 that he reached the conclusion that Ireland must have a parliament of its own. In October of that year he joined the Repeal Association, where he was soon accorded a position second only to that of O'Connell. This must be regarded as a tribute to his social status and his name rather than to his ability. The Repealers were naturally pleased at having attracted into their ranks a Protestant landlord, and one who could claim descent from the eleventh-century hero, Brian Boru; but Smith O'Brien, though honest, enthusiastic and courageous, possessed few of the qualities necessary for political leadership. He was sincerely anxious to promote the welfare of his country; but he was incapable of devising any clear and practicable line of action, and he followed, rather than directed, the course of events. In 1848, moved partly by the example of revolution in France, partly by despair at famine in Ireland, he tried to rouse the peasantry to rebellion. It was a move for which he had made no preparations. He had no arms, no supplies, no assurance of help from any quarter, no plan of campaign. The rebellion collapsed before it had well begun; and he himself was speedily arrested. He was tried for high treason, found guilty and sentenced to death; but the sentence was commuted to one of transportation; and he spent the next six years in Tasmania.

Smith O'Brien's memory is most commonly associated with the abortive insurrection of 1848; but this was a very untypical episode in his career. A few months earlier, he had been foremost in condemning any proposal to employ armed force for the assertion of national rights; and, once the brief excitement of the 'Year of Revolution' had passed, he resumed his old way of thinking. After his return to Ireland in 1856, when he received an unconditional pardon, he used his influence in support of constitutional politics and condemned the violent methods advocated by the Fenians. He was, in fact, a reformer rather than a revolutionary; and he would have remained satisfied with the parliamentary union had he been convinced that it was working to the advantage of

Ireland. There were a good many other Anglo-Irish landlords, in his own day and later, who were equally critical of the government's Irish policy; but there were very few of them who were prepared to do as he did and join forces with the Catholic majority in demanding the re-establishment of a separate Irish parliament.

Thomas Davis, though his career was much briefer than Smith O'Brien's, exercised a wider and more enduring influence; it was an influence that depended on character and ability, not on inherited status. He belonged to that professional middle class, which, from the time of Swift, had been one of the main channels of the Anglo-Irish tradition. It was a tradition of which Davis was both conscious and proud. He was determined that the Anglo-Irish should not be regarded as less than genuine Irishmen, merely on account of religion or descent: though he had been born and educated in Ireland, his father was English; and his mother, through whom he traced his Irish ancestry, was the descendant of a Cromwellian settler. His aim was to proclaim an all-embracing nationality in which the Anglo-Irish could share fully, without any risk of being submerged under a Catholic majority. It was natural, then, that he should look back to Tone and the United Irishmen, who had held similar views; but he was influenced also, and perhaps to a greater extent, by the romantic nationalism of which Mazzini was the prophet. He was not content to base Ireland's claim on any abstract principle, but appealed instead to the record of the past. He constantly advocated the study of Irish history as a means of promoting national self-consciousness; and in that history he himself could always find what he knew in advance must be there, the story of a nation struggling to be free.

Davis's reading of history was selective and tendentious; but the lessons that he drew from it were lessons that Irishmen would have done well to learn. He believed, above all else, that there must be mutual understanding and forbearance between men of different faiths, different traditions, different classes; and during the last five years of his short life he preached incessantly that all other considerations must give way to the necessity for national unity. In doing so, he seemed almost to erect nationalism itself into a kind of religion; and he certainly reduced the age-old differences between the churches to mere matters of private conscience. This was an attitude that accorded well with his own Protestant liberalism; but it could hardly be acceptable to the Roman Catholic bishops. The realities of the situation were revealed in 1845, the last year of his life. The government, anxious to make higher education more generally available in Ireland, established three university colleges—the

Queen's Colleges—on a strictly non-sectarian basis. Davis and his colleagues in the 'Young Ireland' group welcomed the scheme, above all else because it would bring Catholic and Protestant students together in institutions free from any denominational atmosphere. But this very prospect caused alarm among the bishops; and O'Connell's support of episcopal demands for a radical change in the constitution of the colleges threatened to split the Repeal movement. Davis died before the issue was settled; but his plea for unity in education failed. The government refused to introduce sectarian restrictions into the colleges and the bishops accordingly placed them under a ban. Thereafter, for more than sixty years, the main stream of the nationalist movement was committed to an unrelenting attack on the kind of non-sectarian education that Davis had so eagerly welcomed as a unifying force in the divided life of Ireland.

It was not only in the field of education that Davis's ideals suffered defeat. The mutual confidence, on which alone the unity he sought could be based, was altogether lacking. Landlords were alarmed for their estates; Protestants in general feared persecution; the Roman Catholic bishops, anxious for the souls of their people, were suspicious of any close association with heretics. The envy, distrust and fear that divided Catholics and Protestants in every walk of life were increased rather than abated by the excitement of the Repeal campaign. Davis's plea for 'a nationality which may embrace Protestant, Catholic and dissenter—Milesian and Cromwellian—the Irishman of a hundred generations and the stranger who is within our gates' might win applause, but it had little effect on people's attitudes. His appeals to history, to reason, to the ideal of national unity, were widely read; but they failed in their purpose, for readers took from them only what accorded with their own convictions and ignored the rest. Later generations, for whom Davis lives not only in his own writings but also, and more memorably, in those of his friend and admirer, Charles Gavan Duffy, judge him rather by what he hoped for than by what he achieved; and this attractive, romantic, able but ineffective young man stands, not inappropriately, as the symbol of something that has never existed—a truly non-sectarian Irish nationalism.

Davis's ideal of a nationalism transcending differences of religion, class and ancestry, and appealing equally to Irishmen of all traditions, did not die with him; and it has often been held up to admiration. But those who have professed to support this ideal have failed to recognize (just as Davis himself failed to recognize) that its realization would involve the negation, not the fulfilment, of the past history of Ireland.

The free and equal co-operation between Catholic and Protestant advocated by Davis proved impossible in politics. But there was one field of activity in which all could work together without any surrender of principle, one field in which the Anglo-Irish could express their sense of national identity, and could co-operate with Irishmen of a different tradition without abandoning their own—the study of Irish history, antiquities and literature. At least as early as the sixteenth century Anglo-Irish scholars had interested themselves in these subjects; and in the course of the eighteenth interest became more widespread and popular. But in Ireland, as elsewhere in Europe, the nineteenth century saw a new quickening of interest in the past and the spread of this interest through a widening section of the population. New societies were founded to promote archaeological research and to publish the results, to collect and preserve traditional music, to publish ancient manuscripts and reprint old texts, to encourage the study of local history. In all this, the Anglo-Irish gentry and professional classes took a leading part. By education, wealth and command of leisure they were well placed to do so; and here, at least, they were able to take their natural place in the community, for they still dominated those classes of society which in England and Scotland were engaged in the same kind of activity.

The concentration on the distant past that marked much of this archaeological and historical work was in keeping with the fashion of the period. Arguments among Irish scholars about the purpose of the famous round towers were paralleled by the near-contemporary disputes in Scotland over the history of the Picts and in England over the nature of the Druidic cult. But it is not altogether fanciful to suppose that Anglo-Irish scholars felt, perhaps subconsciously, that the further back they went the safer they were. They could be enthusiastic over the valour of ancient Gaelic heroes and the piety of the Celtic church without raising issues that might have an obvious relevance to their own day. Nineteenth-century Irishmen, Catholic and Protestant, Anglo-Irish and Gael, could find in the remote past both a common source of interest and a common ground for pride. Brian Boru's victory at Clontarf in 1014 was free from the implications inseparable from the famous battles of a later period—it was a victory of which all Irishmen could safely be proud, for no party in Ireland had a traditional sympathy with the defeated.

But this study of Gaelic antiquity proved more potent and more divisive than those who encouraged it could have foreseen. The popular imagination was caught by the picture of a glorious past, of an Ireland with a distinctive culture of its own, untouched by English influence; and the very vagueness of the outline left the imagination free to shape the picture as it would. From this cloudy but exciting concept of a golden and heroic age sprang the idea of a Gaelic nationality, of an Ireland that would reject not only English power but English culture and express its independence not only in its own government but its own language.

In preparing the way for this development Anglo-Irish writers played a major part. Though they had no political purpose, they could neither restrain nor control the force they had released; and they contributed, unwittingly, to the downfall of their own tradition. The ideal of a Gaelic Ireland bred an attitude conducive to cultural, and even to racial, exclusiveness. In time, the bounds of Irish nationality became even more narrowly drawn; and when the opportunity came, in the 1920s, Irishmen set to work to build up a Gaelic nation guided by the social teaching of the Roman Catholic church. It was a nation in which the Anglo-Irish tradition could subsist, if at all, only on sufferance.

(4)

The attachment of the Anglo-Irish to the parliamentary union was the product of circumstances. Their permanent and essential characteristic was their Protestantism; and even those of them who joined the nationalist cause remained a distinct element within it, unless, as some of them did, they abandoned their hereditary faith as well as their hereditary politics. The Protestantism of the Anglo-Irish was that of the established church, the Church of Ireland—indeed, in normal Irish usage of the period the term 'Protestant' was used in this restricted sense: it meant a member of the Church of Ireland, as distinct from a Roman Catholic, on the one hand, or a Presbyterian, on the other. This threefold division of the population had much more than a merely ecclesiastical significance, It reflected a division in cultural tradition as well as in religious faith; and nineteenth-century Ireland failed to produce any leader who could combine the diverse cultures in a common cause.

The emergence of a strong and aggressive Catholic nationalism brought with it a threat to the Church of Ireland. Its position as the established church of the country had been specifically guaranteed by the act of union. But it was unlikely that any guarantee could stand indefinitely in face of popular agitation for disestablishment and disendowment; and in 1869, just forty years after the admission of Roman Catholics to parliament, the Irish Church Act disestablished the church and confiscated almost the whole of its property. At the time, this was seen by the Anglo-Irish as a black betrayal: the Church of Ireland was their church; and the permanent preservation of its status and rights had been one of the fundamental conditions on which they had accepted the parliamentary union. In fact, however, this seeming disaster turned to the advantage of the church and, so far from weakening it, made it stronger than before.

The attachment of the Anglo-Irish to their church had taken on a new character as a result of the union with Great Britain; for now that they no longer had a parliament of their own the church stood as the most important symbol of their corporate entity. Nominally, it is true, the Church of Ireland was no longer a distinct body: the act of union had provided that it should be merged with the Church of England, in a single 'United Church of England and Ireland'. But this statutory union had no real effect. On the title-page of the Prayer Book and in the language of lawyers the United Church had a kind of shadowy existence; but in the public mind and in ordinary speech the Church of Ireland and the Church of England remained distinct—identical in doctrine and usage, but each with its own tradition and its own life. When disestablishment brought even the nominal union between the churches to an end Irish churchmen could accept the separation without feeling that there had been any essential breach of continuity with the past.

The part that the church played in the life of the Anglo-Irish during the period of the union, and later, would hardly have been possible had not the church itself undergone a considerable change in character and outlook since the eighteenth century. It is true that the eighteenth-century church was not quite the spiritual desert that some accounts would suggest. The bishops and the parochial clergy included many men of piety and learning who took their duties seriously. The frequent publication of sermons and other religious works shows that there was an extensive demand for reading of this kind. Among clergy and laity alike there was a good deal of concern about the promotion of charitable causes. But the general picture is, at best, one of drab respectability and conventional conformity; and even these virtues were often lacking. Promotion to higher office depended almost entirely on political interest, with scant regard for fitness; and the church was commonly regarded as little more than a department of state. Even before the union, however, the Church of Ireland had begun to feel the impact of the Evangelical revival that was already at work in the Church of England; and this Evangelical influence was to transform the life of the church and give it a new sense of unity and purpose. The change had not only a religious but also a social significance. In founding and directing the numerous societies and institutions to which the

Evangelical influence gave rise laymen played a very active part; and the notion that religion was the business of the laity as well as the clergy grew stronger and more widespread, even among laymen who were little affected by Evangelical theology. In this way, a sense of corporate identity, embracing the whole membership of the church, grew stronger; and in time it made the Church of Ireland a natural channel for the expression of the views of the Anglo-Irish community as a whole.

Throughout the nineteenth century, and beyond, the Evangelical influence remained dominant, partly because Tractarianism, which in England provided a counter-attraction, had few followers in Ireland, partly because the Evangelical leaders, especially in the early decades of the century, were men of great ability and strength of character, and distinguished for learning as well as for zeal. A large proportion of them came from the upper ranks of society. Peter Roe, often regarded as the patriarch of the movement, belonged to one of the wealthiest families in Dublin—it was his cousin, Henry Roe, who later devoted a fortune to the restoration of Christ Church Cathedral. His contemporaries and successors among the clergy included members of many of the most distinguished Anglo-Irish families: Edward and William Wingfield, Denis Browne, Fitzwilliam Trench, Hans Caulfield, Robert Daly, William Bushe, Thomas de Burgh. The many prominent laymen who supported the movement, by their gifts and by their labours, were widely representative of the rank, wealth and ability of the country. It is hardly surprising that James Anthony Froude, who had been taught at Oxford to regard Evangelicals as 'weak, amiable, but silly persons, without learning or judgement', should have been surprised to find, on his first visit to Ireland, that an Evangelical might also be a scholar and a gentleman, 'with the easy dignity of high breeding'.

These Irish Evangelicals were much concerned about social conditions and were always ready to devote time and money to the relief of poverty. But their greatest and most urgent desire was to propagate the Scriptures among the Roman Catholic population. It was chiefly with this end in view that they were so active in setting up schools where the reading of the Bible was a regular part of every day's instruction. Many of them engaged also in a more direct form of missionary activity; and for this purpose they encouraged the study of the Irish language, through which they hoped that they might more readily make contact with the large Irish-speaking population that still existed, especially in the west. Robert Daly edited an Irish-English dictionary; Henry Monck Mason, an Evangelical lawyer and antiquary, was largely instrumental in establishing a chair of Irish in Trinity College; and earlier, in 1818, a group of clergy and laity had founded a society specially devoted to the employment of the Irish language in the work of conversion. All over the country, earnest missionaries preached, persuaded and argued, distributed Bibles and tracts, and challenged the Roman Catholic clergy to public debates on controverted points of divinity.

What degree of success attended all this effort is a matter of some doubt; but it was sufficient to arouse the alarm of the Roman Catholic clergy. They directed their principal attack against the practice of unrestricted Bible-reading in schools, and especially in the schools of the Kildare Place Society. This had been founded as a non-denominational body, with both Roman Catholic and Protestant support; and it received an annual grant from the government. But growing Evangelical influence in the society alienated the Roman Catholic authorities; and under pressure from them the government changed its policy. In 1831, the annual grant was transferred to a new body, the Commissioners of National Education; and the commissioners withheld support from any school in which Bible-reading was a regular and compulsory part of the curriculum. The reaction of the Church of Ireland clergy to this new rule indicates the strength of Evangelical influence. The great majority refused to accept support on these terms, preferring to retain their liberty and to rely on voluntary subscriptions. To many of them, this line of action meant a considerable personal sacrifice; for it was government policy not to appoint to a crown living, still less to a deanery or bishopric, any clergyman who opposed the new educational system.

Behind the missionary activity of the Evangelical clergy, behind their insistence on liberty to have the Bible read by all who attended their schools, was a firm belief that their first duty to Ireland was to promote Protestantism, or, as they themselves would have expressed it, 'to spread the Gospel'. This was the great national cause, to which, as Irishmen and as ministers of the established church, they were bound to devote themselves. It was an expression of national feeling unlikely to be popular with the majority. The Church of Ireland was traditionally regarded as alien; those who abandoned their hereditary faith in order to conform were looked on as traitors, their motives called in question and they themselves subjected to all the hostile pressures that a closely knit community could exert. From time to time, popular disapproval expressed itself in more violent ways: those who engaged in the work of propaganda were not unlikely to be stoned; and they were warned, by an occasional example, that they could not ignore the risk of being murdered.

It is easy to see this missionary activity as an attempt by the Church of Ireland to bolster up its position in face of the growing political influence of Roman Catholicism; and the way in which over-optimistic estimates of its success were used in defence of the establishment gives some colour to this view. But the roots of the missionary enterprise ran much deeper. Evangelical teaching bred a strong, sometimes an overpowering, sense of responsibility for the souls of one's neighbours; and among Evangelical clergy of the Church of Ireland this was reinforced by the conviction that they were representatives of a national church with a mission to the whole people, irrespective of denomination: it is significant that many of them were quite as earnest in their efforts to win over dissenters as in their efforts to win over Roman Catholics. In short, they felt themselves to be engaged in a great task for the glory of God and the welfare of Ireland. It was a kind of patriotism that brought them little honour in this world, however it may be judged in the next.

By no means all the clergy of the Church of Ireland shared the Evangelical outlook. But, even among those who did not, Evangelical influence and example had a widespread effect in raising the general standard of attention to duty and implanting a stronger sense of responsibility. Though there were many, even among the Evangelicals, who doubted the wisdom of direct and open missionary activity, the doubt related rather to the means than to the end; and the conviction that the church was a national institution, with a duty to the whole population, was probably more widely held during the last few decades before disestablishment than at any earlier period. This is not to say that all the old abuses in the ecclesiastical system had been remedied, or that the ideals of the Evangelical leaders had been fully realized, even by those who professed to accept them. But there was certainly a much greater awareness than formerly of the church's function as a divine society acting under a higher authority than that of the state.

The total effect of the Evangelical influence on the Irish church has been very variously assessed, but of one thing there can be no doubt: it was the Evangelical movement that brought the laity into active participation in the church's work. In a wide range of societies and activities, national and parochial, laymen were actively involved, thus acquiring a strong sense of membership and responsibility. Occasionally, also, they developed a sense of independence from settled ecclesiastical authority: it was in a group of such earnest but anti-clerical laymen, meeting in Dublin, that the organization later to be known as the Plymouth Brethren had its origin. But Irish laymen in general were loyal to the church; and it was their loyalty that made it possible for the church not only to survive the crisis of disestablishment but to emerge from it stronger than before. It is true that the church population declined, with the general decline in the population of Ireland; but it rose as a proportion of the whole. And in some areas there was a rise in absolute numbers: in Connemara, for example, the Protestant population in 1881 was not far short of twice what it had been twenty years earlier. All over the country, the restoration of old churches and the building of new ones expressed the zeal and generosity of the people and their confidence in the future.

Disestablishment brought with it, almost of necessity, a greater participation of laymen in the direction of ecclesiastical affairs. The church was now governed by a 'General Synod' of two houses, one consisting of the bishops, the other of representatives of the parochial clergy and of the laity. In the working of the new constitution, especially during the first generation after disestablishment, the lay influence was predominantly that of the landed and professional classes; and since the clergy also were drawn, to a large extent, from the same classes, it is hardly surprising to find that a roll-call of the general synod is reminiscent of a roll-call of the old Irish parliament. Once again, the Anglo-Irish had an assembly of their own, in which they could make speeches and pass legislation, though their business now concerned only the domestic affairs of a disestablished church. But it was an assembly that could be used, on occasion, for the expression of political views; and in 1886, 1893 and 1912 the synod declared its total opposition to the policy of Home Rule. In the synod in 1893 the attitude of the Anglo-Irish was succinctly summed up by Lord Plunket, the archbishop of Dublin:

> It is because we are patriots and because we love our country that we protest with all the energy and all the indignation of our nature against a bill which, if carried into effect, would inflict upon our native land financial ruin, national degradation, intestine strife, and, it may be, civil war.

The episode has a greater significance than might at first appear, for the speaker was a grandson of the Plunket who had spoken so fiercely against union less than a century earlier. Such was the change that time and circumstances had worked in the outlook of the Anglo-Irish.

The Protestantism of the Anglo-Irish, though closely associated with their attachment to the parliamentary union, contained an element of ecclesiastical nationalism. Their attitude to the church may be seen as a parallel to their former attitude to the Kingdom of Ireland. In the seventeenth and eighteenth centuries they had based their constitutional claims on an assumption of national continuity, stretching back even beyond the first arrival of the Anglo-Normans; and they applied this assumption of continuity to the Church of Ireland as well. It was not, as the Roman Catholics alleged, an alien institution imported into the country by English authority in the sixteenth century. It was the ancient church of St. Patrick, reformed and purified, but still essentially the same, still the national church, even though the great bulk of the population had rejected it. This was not, of course, a new claim, though in the decades before and after disestablishment, when the church was under strong attack, it was asserted with a new emphasis. Its spirit is caught in a popular rhyme, which probably dates from the eighteenth century:

> *St. Patrick was a gentleman;*
> *He came of decent people;*
> *He built a church in Dublin town*
> *And on it put a steeple.*

The words are neutral; but the provenance of the rhyme is strictly Protestant; and, at least by implication, it claims for the Church of Ireland both St. Patrick himself and the great medieval church that bears his name, St. Patrick's Cathedral. For the Anglo-Irish, this is the central shrine of their church and a symbol of its identity, continuity and status. Built in the thirteenth century, but linked by name and tradition with the apostle of Ireland, it is associated with great names and great events. From the walls of the choir, formerly the chapel of the Knights of St. Patrick, hang the banners of the most famous Anglo-Irish families. Here, if anywhere, the Anglo-Irish could indulge in a sense of national pride, supported by history and justified by great achievement. Here they could feel that they were indeed Irishmen, heirs and guardians of a truly national tradition, binding them together in a common allegiance.

This ecclesiastical nationalism did nothing to separate the Church of Ireland from the rest of the Anglican Communion. Its bishops took their place in successive Lambeth Conferences; and it willingly recognized the traditional primacy of honour belonging to the see of Canterbury. And it retained and revered that most typical expression of English religious feeling, at once fervent and restrained, the Book of Common Prayer. One can see some similarity, though the emphasis is rather different, between the outlook of the Anglo-Irish in the ecclesiastical sphere and their conception of their place in the United Kingdom and the Empire. Though proud of their own country and their own tradition, they never saw either in isolation but always in some wider setting, the world-wide Anglican Communion or the almost equally extensive British Empire. Wherever the church or the flag or the businessman might go, they were ready either to lead or to follow. The missionaries who set off for Africa or India, for China or Japan or South America, though far less numerous than the stream of sailors and soldiers, civil servants and traders, who followed the same routes, were no less a part of the great nineteenth-century expansion of an English culture that had transcended its national origins and become a world force. To the Irish nationalist, these men, whether their mission was ecclesiastical or military or civil, might seem to have abandoned their birthright, to have taken service with an alien church, an alien culture, an alien power; but to the Anglo-Irish this was the way in which Ireland could best achieve true greatness and best fulfil a noble purpose in the world.

The disestablishment of the Church of Ireland might appear at first sight a comparatively unimportant episode. For the Irish majority, certainly, it meant the removal of a longstanding grievance; but the grievance had been symbolic rather than real; and its removal made little practical difference. For those who suffered by disestablishment the situation was, of course, different. But they were in no position to fight back; their only course was to accept the change and adjust themselves to the new situation, which they did with great courage and remarkable rapidity. Within a few years, the whole affair was, in the general opinion, over and done with. But disestablishment was far more significant than appearances would suggest. It marks the first open surrender to the claims of Catholic nationalism, the first clear and unmistakable step towards the British government's abandonment of the Anglo-Irish. This was a road on which there could be no turning back, though half a century was to pass before its end, already implicit in its beginning, was to be reached.

VI

Surrender

(1)

In the history of the Anglo-Irish the disestablishment of the church is more important as an omen than for its practical effects. But, almost at the same time, there arose in Ireland a movement that was to give new force to popular demands, to change radically the attitude of British governments towards Ireland and, in the end, to prepare the way for the destruction of the Anglo-Irish community.

In the origins of the movement there was little to suggest that its future course would lead to such a result. Its founder, Isaac Butt, came from a typical Anglo-Irish background—he was the son of a country rector, educated at Raphoe Royal School, in his native Donegal, and at Trinity College, Dublin. Though the strong Toryism that he showed in early life became somewhat less rigid later on, his outlook remained conservative; and he was a convinced supporter of the parliamentary union. But his experience as an M.P. had persuaded him that the union might, with advantage, be modified. He thought that Irish business was often neglected or mismanaged at Westminster and that it should therefore be transferred to a subordinate legislature in Dublin. But the union would remain intact: supreme authority would still rest with the British parliament, in which Ireland would continue to be represented as before. Butt published his proposals in 1869; and from this beginning sprang the 'Home Rule' movement that dominated Irish politics for almost half a century.

Within a short time this new movement was to deepen still further the sectarian cleavage in Ireland and to threaten the Anglo-Irish, as they believed, with total destruction. But its early character was very different; and Protestants, so far from being alarmed, were inclined to regard it with favour. Butt, after all, was one of themselves; and he had made his political reputation as an opponent of O'Connell. He insisted that the Home Rule cause must be kept free from all party and sectarian ties; it was to be a cause in which Irishmen of all traditions could join, and those who supported it would not be committed to anything beyond the establishment of a subordinate Irish parliament. And Butt launched his proposals just at a time when Irish Protestants were politically unsettled. Gladstone was clearly their enemy, intent on placating the Roman Catholics at their expense; and the Conservatives, on whom they were wont to rely, had been little more than lukewarm in their defence. They were in a mood to try something new; and the risk seemed a limited one. Home Rule was not Repeal; and, if the worst came to the worst, the Protestant majority at Westminster would outweigh a Roman Catholic majority in Dublin. It is not, then, surprising to find Protestants foremost among the early supporters of the Home Rule movement that they were later to denounce so bitterly.

It was ominous for the future that this Protestant support aroused suspicion among Roman Catholics. The *Freeman's Journal* warned its readers against 'this insidious attempt made to seduce them from their allegiance to their country and drag them into the mire of Toryism'; but the warning was hardly needed: a few by-elections were enough to show that Roman Catholic voters would not support a candidate who had no policy to offer beyond an alliance of creeds and classes in the cause of Home Rule. If the movement was to prosper it must abandon Butt's principles; it must ally itself with the tenant against the landlord and it must win the co-operation of the Roman Catholic clergy. Within a very few years the transformation was complete. Butt's vision of a national union transcending sectarian and sectional interests dissolved and vanished. Protestant support fell away; and what was left was a Home Rule party committed to agrarian reform and heavily dependent on the Roman Catholic church. It continued to attract the support of individual Protestants and for a long time it relied on Protestant leadership; but it became and remained the party of the Roman Catholic population.

The Catholic character that the Home Rule movement so quickly assumed was not merely negative, the result of Protestant withdrawal; it was positive and deliberate. The party needed the support of Catholic voters, who formed the great majority of the electorate; it could not count on this support unless it had the co-operation of the clergy; and clerical co-operation imposed conditions that Protestants in general could hardly be expected to accept. On denominational issues, especially in the field of education, the party must make the Catholic cause its own; and in such matters it regularly followed the line laid down for it by the Roman Catholic bishops, and put forward their claims as representing the national will of the Irish people. To an outsider, it might seem reasonable enough that the majority should have its way; but to Irish Protestants the policy followed by the party seemed a clear indication that there would be little room for them in an Ireland governed by Home Rule politicians.

Though the sectarianism of the Home Rule movement was a necessary condition of its alliance with the church, it had deeper roots also. Among Roman Catholics in general there was a widespread belief that Protestants represented an alien element in the country. Those of them who took up the cause of the majority might be welcomed and made much of; but Ireland was and must remain a Catholic nation; and Protestants, if they wished to be considered as Irishmen at all, must accept this fact. The politics of Catholic Ireland were not to be secularized for the sake of a minority group descended from foreign settlers, whose tyrannical control the nation was still struggling to throw off. This attitude was to be strengthened, and given a new dimension, by the Gaelic revival later in the nineteenth century; but it can be traced far into the past, to the Confederate Catholics of the 1640s, and beyond. Implicit in all this was a problem of national identity. Was the 'Irish nation' con-terminous with the whole population? Or was it some smaller group, to which a man belonged by right of descent, or religion, or political commitment? Few people were willing to recognize the difficulties that these questions raised; but they could not be got rid of by ignoring them; and later generations were to suffer by the refusal of the Home Rule party to face the realities of the situation.

This problem of national identity was not implicit in the policy of Home Rule, as defined by Butt. That policy was not strictly 'nationalist' at all, for it laid no claim to national independence, and, in any case, Butt took the view, held by the Anglo-Irish in general, that those born in Ireland were Irishmen, irrespective of descent, religion or politics. But, even before Butt's death, a new spirit had invaded the Home Rule party and soon came to dominate it. Formal policy remained unchanged; and party leaders, when seeking support in Britain, generally thought it wise to emphasize the modesty of their aims. But when they stood on their own soil and addressed their own people their tone changed. Then they would fiercely denounce the iniquities of 'foreign' rule and stir up memories of ancient conflict, not without prophecies of a day, soon to come, when wrongs would be redressed and former glories restored, when Ireland would take her proper place in the world, 'a nation once again'. By other means also the same spirit found expression—in songs, newspapers and books, all inculcating the same lesson, that Ireland must be freed from English tyranny. Protestants found it hard to believe that those who preached such doctrines would long rest satisfied with a subordinate legislature in Dublin; instead, they would use it as a stepping-stone to total separation. And an independent Ireland, governed in the spirit of this popular propaganda, would hardly be an Ireland in which Protestants could feel themselves comfortably at home.

The divisive influence of the Catholic nationalism that the Home Rule party embodied and propagated was felt throughout Ireland; and it was felt with even greater force after the electoral reforms of 1884 and 1885 had increased and consolidated the party's voting strength. Over most of the country Protestants now found themselves excluded, even more completely than before, from any share in parliamentary politics, unless, as a few did, they supported the Home Rule cause and all that it stood for. Only in the north was the Protestant vote still strong enough to be important; and it was in the north that the divisive influence of Home Rule policy was most obvious at the time and most significant for the future. It might, perhaps, have seemed possible that the agrarian programme on which the party always laid great stress would draw together Protestant and Catholic tenants, who were equally interested in improving their conditions of tenure; but the party leaders knew that they could not come to terms with the Protestants and at the same time maintain the denominational policies required by their alliance with the church. Though they made occasional appeals for unity, they devoted their main efforts to organizing effectively the Catholic vote in those Ulster constituencies where it might be strong enough to enable them to win. These tactics inevitably emphasized rather than allayed the force of the sectarian division; and Protestants were confirmed in their belief that Home Rule was a Catholic cause, where there was no room for Protestants, save on Catholic terms. This inability of the Home Rule movement to escape from its denominational framework helped to prepare the way for the later partition of the country, with all that this was to mean for the Protestants of the south and west, the true heirs of the Anglo-Irish tradition.

It might appear, at first sight, something of an anomaly that the Home Rule movement, with its strongly Catholic character, should not only have had a Protestant as its founder, but should also have had a Protestant as its greatest leader, Charles Stewart Parnell. In fact, however, Butt and Parnell were only two in a long line of Protestants who, from the eighteenth century onwards, provided Catholic Ireland with a leadership that it seemed incapable of providing for itself. The Anglo-Irish were often arrogant and narrow-minded, they often wore their Protestantism as a badge of superiority, but in every generation they produced men who

were ready to set at risk the interests of their own community for the sake
of what they regarded as a nobler cause. These men were generally
concerned to break down denominational barriers and to create a concept
of nationality that would embrace the whole people. Tone and Davis and
Butt himself all had this end in view. But Parnell, though he spoke
occasionally of the contribution that Protestants could and should make to
the life of Ireland, did nothing to promote that mutual understanding
between conflicting groups that was so often the theme of other Protestant
nationalists. It is hard to assess with any confidence the motives that
guided this strange man, who is an enigma to historians as he was to
contemporaries. His nationalism had none of the romantic fervour that
characterized so many Home Rule politicians—Irish history, Irish
literature, the Irish language had little interest for him. No one else, except
O'Connell, has ever exercised such a widespread and dominating influence
in Ireland; yet the two men were utterly unlike, not only in personal
character, but also in the nature of their appeal. If we are to compare
Parnell with anyone it must be with Swift. In spite of all that separates
them, there is a recognizable kinship; and each represents, in his own way,
the Anglo-Irish spirit in revolt.

Parnell's main achievement was to impose upon the Home Rule party
the effective organization and firm discipline that it had hitherto lacked;
and his success in doing so was clearly shown in the general election of
1885, when the party won over eighty per cent of the Irish seats. The
significance of this victory was greatly increased by the state of politics
in Great Britain. The Liberals, under Gladstone, had emerged from the
election as the largest single party; but their lead over the Conservatives
was exactly equalled by the strength of the Home Rulers. If Gladstone
was to unseat the Conservative government then in office and form a
Liberal ministry he must have the support of Parnell. From this situation
sprang an informal alliance between Liberals and Home Rulers; and the
Liberal party was thenceforth committed to a policy of Home Rule for
Ireland.

It is hardly too much to say that this alliance settled the fate of the
Anglo-Irish, even though that fate was to be delayed for more than a
generation. Hitherto, the bedrock of their security had been the solid
determination of Great Britain to maintain the union unchanged. Now
that solidarity had been broken; the maintenance of the union had ceased
to be a basic assumption of British politics and had become an open issue
between the parties. It was an issue that could, in the long run, be resolved

in one way only. The Home Rulers, encouraged by the support of the Liberal party, would never relax their claims. The Liberals might, from time to time, allow Home Rule to fall into the background of their programme; but they would always return to it when they needed the votes of the Irish members. Sooner or later, whether by Liberal victory or Conservative change of heart, or by agreement between the two parties, a separate parliament would be set up for Ireland; and the Anglo-Irish community would be left defenceless. The hatred with which Gladstone was long regarded by Irish Protestants arose less from his disestablishment and disendowment of the church than from his readiness to betray (as they would have expressed it) Protestant Ireland into the hands of the enemy.*

The threat that faced the Anglo-Irish in 1886 was temporarily averted. Gladstone's decision to support Home Rule split his own party and opened the way for a long period of Conservative domination; and, while their friends were in power, the Anglo-Irish could feel safe. But it was a precarious safety, that might at any time be threatened by a change of electoral fortunes; and the Anglo-Irish, alert to the danger that faced them, had already begun to organize in their own defence.

(2)

The events of 1885–6 proved a turning-point in the history of the Anglo-Irish, not just because of the Liberal conversion to Home Rule but also because it was at this point that they first made a concerted effort to establish and maintain a distinct political organization of their own. Hitherto, they had allowed themselves to be absorbed into the main stream of British politics, where, for the most part, they had tended to support the Conservatives, though there also survived a small, but not negligible, Liberal (or, at least, Whiggish) interest. On occasion, of course, their attitude had been strongly influenced by the Irish situation; but Ireland had not been the centre of their political life nor the dominating factor in their political conduct. In 1885–6 all this was to undergo a change; and the change, originally stimulated by the growing menace of the Home Rule movement, was confirmed by the change in the Liberal party's Irish policy.

The organization through which the Anglo-Irish hoped to strengthen their resistance to the policy of Home Rule was the Irish Loyal and

* In some Irish country houses one may still be shown a striking memento of this hatred—a chamber-pot with a portrait of Gladstone in the bottom.

Patriotic Union, founded in 1885 in preparation for the general election of that year; and it survived—though its name was later changed to the Irish Unionist Alliance—until the 1920s. By its constitution it was to be a non-sectarian body, and it did, in fact, attract a few Roman Catholic supporters; but its founders were, for the most part, prominent members of the Church of Ireland; and, throughout its history, it sought to represent the special interests of the Protestant population of the three southern provinces. It was, in short, an embodiment of the typical political outlook of the Anglo-Irish. The founders of the I.L.P.U. had no idea of establishing a new party. They simply agreed to sink their political differences, ignore the distinction between Conservative and Liberal, and support candidates pledged to defend the parliamentary union. The election of 1885 showed how narrow was the basis on which their organization stood. Not one of its fifty-two candidates was elected; and they received, on an average, only ten per cent of the votes cast. But this figure was itself significant, for it corresponded almost precisely to the Protestant proportion of the population in the southern provinces. If the election result demonstrated the hopelessness of contesting seats it also gave a strong indication that the rank and file of the Anglo-Irish were solidly behind their leaders in opposition to Home Rule. This solidarity, though of little electoral consequence, was yet a matter of importance. A distinctive and self-conscious minority, numbering some ten per cent of the population, had at least a good claim to have its voice heard and its interests protected.

There was, of course, very little risk that the Anglo-Irish would not be heard, for their leaders were well placed to command public attention. They were men of rank and wealth, often with property or business interests in England as well as in Ireland; they were strongly represented in the House of Lords; and a significant number of them sat for British constituencies in the House of Commons. Their main reliance was on the Conservative party, within which they were able to exercise a very powerful influence. Indeed, maintenance of the union was such an essential element in Conservative policy that, in time, 'Unionist' and 'Conservative' became interchangeable terms. The Anglo-Irish, then, had available the means of putting their case before the British electors; and they had, also, the ability and the financial resources to use those means to the full.

To the majority of their fellow-countrymen the attitude they took and the policy they followed seemed to be simply 'anti-Irish', a kind of treason against the nation. But they themselves believed that in opposing Home Rule they were performing a patriotic duty: the prosperity of

Ireland, no less than their own security, depended on the maintenance of the union. And this view could co-exist not only with a genuine concern for the welfare of the country, but also with an enthusiastic interest in its ancient history and culture—Standish James O'Grady, whose *History of Ireland* was one of the main sources of the Gaelic revival, was also a vigorous writer in support of the Unionist cause. Sir Horace Plunkett, though a Unionist himself, complained that Unionists in general did not do nearly enough to promote, in non-political ways, the economic and social betterment of the people; and his complaints were not unfounded. But political divisions were so strongly marked that it was almost impossible to keep politics out of any kind of public activity; and help or guidance, however disinterested, was rarely welcomed from anyone who was a known opponent of Home Rule. Even Plunkett's own experience might have shown him this; for his co-operative movement, though it achieved a substantial measure of success, was hampered from the beginning by the popular suspicion, encouraged by some Roman Catholic clergy and some politicians, that no good thing could come from a man who was at once a Protestant, a landlord and a Unionist. The Anglo-Irish landlords, industrialists and businessmen, against whom Plunkett's complaints were directed, certainly did less than they might have done for the common good. But the fault was not entirely theirs; and, even if they had been as conscientious as Plunkett desired, the outcome of the struggle would hardly have been affected. The emerging Catholic Nation did not want their services except on its own terms.

In retrospect, then, the cause of the Anglo-Irish may well seem to have been hopeless from the beginning. But throughout most of the period between the first Home Rule bill in 1885 and the signing of the Treaty in 1921 they themselves were full of confidence; and there were some who retained this confidence to the end and to whom the final defeat came as a bitter shock. This confident attitude need not, when all the circumstances are considered, appear surprising. The split in the Liberal party and the sweeping Conservative victory in the general election of 1886 convinced the Anglo-Irish that, come what might, the people of Great Britain would always, in the end, stand by the union. It was a period of rising pride in the Empire—a pride that the Anglo-Irish themselves fully shared—and any tampering with the union could easily be represented as an attack upon the Empire at its centre. As for the strength of Home Rule feeling in Ireland, the Anglo-Irish had persuaded themselves and tried to persuade the British electorate that it had been grossly exaggerated, that the bulk of the Roman Catholic population was really quite satisfied with British rule and was being misled and bullied by an alliance of priests and politicians. If only the government stood firm, people would sooner or later come to their senses and throw off the folly of Home Rule.

Underlying the confidence of the Anglo-Irish was another element, which is less easy to define, but no less important. They had inherited from the past a firm belief in their own superiority to the Catholic population, a superiority that was, in their minds, sufficient to compensate for their lack of numbers and to entitle them, as a community, to at least an equal voice in determining the fate of Ireland. This belief has its most obvious basis in the fact that Protestants formed such a high proportion of the well-to-do classes. Not only were the landlords predominantly Protestant, but among professional men and among the leaders of commerce and industry the number of Protestants was out of all proportion to the strength of the Protestant population as a whole. Even at a much lower level, Protestantism and prosperity seemed to go together. In many a country town where Protestants formed only a tiny proportion of the population they owned the most flourishing businesses and lived in the best houses; and, lower still, the Protestant workman commonly regarded himself, and was sometimes regarded by others, as marked off from his Catholic mates by superior cleanliness, honesty and industry.

This Protestant sense of distinctiveness and superiority is reflected in some of the Anglo-Irish novelists of the period; and the fact that it is more often assumed than openly expressed emphasizes its pervasive influence. In the stories of Somerville and Ross the distinction might appear to be one of class rather than of creed; but the connection between the two is never far below the surface. It is for example hard to imagine that Charlotte Mullin, in *The Real Charlotte*, would ever have reached even the doubtful place she held on the fringe of county society if she had been a Roman Catholic instead of a Protestant. In the novels of George A. Birmingham, where the social range is wider and distinctions of class less strongly marked, the idea of a natural Protestant superiority, independent of position or wealth, comes out more clearly; and even in his most sympathetic portraits of Catholic characters one can detect an air of condescension. This notion of a Protestant superiority is not, of course, confined to works of fiction; and it can crop up in unexpected places, as, for example, in Sean O'Casey's autobiographical account of his childhood in a Dublin slum. The family was Protestant; and his mother refused to sink to the level of her neighbours. By ceaseless labour she contrived to keep herself and her children, and the wretched rooms in which they lived, clean and free from vermin. And O'Casey himself, just because he was a Protestant, started life in a much better job than would have been likely to fall in the way of a Catholic boy from the same sort of background. Protestant slum-dwellers must have been so rare that O'Casey's experience cannot be taken as typical. But the emphasis that he himself lays on the importance of the Protestant influence in his early life can hardly be ignored. The material advantages associated with being a Protestant could extend to the very bottom of the social scale.

Neither the Irish Loyal and Patriotic Union nor the Irish Unionist Alliance which succeeded it ever achieved a large popular membership among the Protestant population of the south and west; and though local branches were established in many places, they did not flourish. There was, in fact, little for a widespread organization to do. It was not needed for electoral purposes: the experiment of putting up a large number of candidates, tried unsuccessfully in 1885, was not repeated, and had, indeed, been little more than a gesture. From time to time, public meetings in support of the union were held in Dublin, and occasionally in other centres also; but these were intended to encourage the faithful, not to win new converts. The real task to which the leaders of the southern Protestants applied themselves was that of maintaining and extending their influence in the Conservative party and of conducting propaganda in Great Britain. The membership of the organizations they established was made up almost entirely of people who were able and willing to support this work by their subscriptions and, very often, by active participation also. Without this concerted and continued effort by men of influence, wealth and ability, the case of the southern Protestants must have gone by default. It would be a mistake to suppose that these men represented nothing more than the special interests of the narrow class from which they were drawn; but there was not much regular communication or contact between them and the hundreds of thousands of humbler people whose future depended on the outcome of their efforts. What held the great body of southern Protestants together and sustained their sense of a corporate distinctiveness was not political organization or political leadership, but the Church of Ireland, to which the great majority of them belonged. When the political battle had been lost and they were handed over to their new masters it was among the bishops of the church that they found their wisest leaders.

The fact that the Unionists of the three southern provinces provided themselves with an organization of their own did not mean that they regarded their interest as different from that of the Unionists of Ulster;

nor did the Ulster Unionists, for their part, start off with any idea of fighting a purely local campaign. Difference of circumstances required difference in organization and tactics; but the two groups had a single common object, to defeat in parliament any proposal to set up a Home Rule legislature in Ireland. Later on, when it began to appear that their joint efforts would not succeed, a majority of Ulster Unionists came to believe that they would do better to desert their allies and make terms for themselves. It was this change of outlook that, in the end, deprived the Anglo-Irish of their last hope of being allowed to play a significant part in the life of their country.

(3)

The dominance of the aristocratic element in the leadership of the southern Unionists strengthened the impression, misleading though it was, that they stood for nothing more than the determination of a small privileged class to defend its own position. But no one could doubt that, in Ulster, Unionism was a popular cause, supported by the majority of the population. The leaders were, as in the south, men of rank and wealth; but their influence depended less on their personal status than on their representative character, and they were obliged to keep in close touch with their followers. The policy of the southern Unionists was decided for them by their leaders; in Ulster, the leaders could move only within the limits prescribed by popular opinion. And this popular opinion had been hardened by the open sectarianism that was such a marked feature of the Home Rule movement in the north. To most Ulster Protestants this sectarianism was a clear warning that they were regarded as aliens, for whom there was no place in the 'Irish nation' that was now so loudly demanding the right to govern itself. This conviction strengthened their resolve to resist Home Rule; but it also prepared them to accept, as a second best, a compromise settlement by which they might save themselves, while leaving the rest of the country to go its own way.

It was only by degrees, and under prompting and pressure from outside, that Ulster Protestants reached this decision. It was a selfish decision, but not an unnatural one. Their Protestantism was so strongly coloured by the Scottish Presbyterian influence that they had no compelling sense of responsibility for the Protestant minority in the south and west. The Anglo-Irish tradition, with its roots in a remote past, made little appeal to most of them. They were willing to accept, even while they resented, the nationalist assumption that 'Irish' and 'Catholic' were interchangeable terms; and, having accepted the assumption, they were ready to act upon it. Rather than be submerged in a Catholic Ireland they would fight for their own Protestant province. From this conflict between Catholic nationalism and Ulster Protestantism arose the partition of Ireland, a result at which no one had aimed but which no one was strong enough to prevent.

Perhaps the southern Unionists, to whose future prospects partition was to prove a fatal blow, should have foreseen the danger. Instead, they regarded the strength of Unionism in Ulster as one of their principal safeguards and believed that Ulster opposition was such a powerful argument against Home Rule that it would help to save all Ireland for the union. They were encouraged in this belief by the fact that for a long time Ulster Unionists themselves shared the same view. Edward Saunderson, for more than twenty years their principal spokesman at Westminster, always considered the interests of Ireland as a whole. If he concentrated attention on Ulster opposition to Home Rule, even to the extent of advocating armed resistance, it was because this seemed to him the ground on which any Home Rule scheme could most readily be defeated. But he rejected out of hand the idea of separating the interests of north and south. When it was suggested, during the debate on the Home Rule bill of 1886, that the establishment of an Irish parliament might be more acceptable if special terms were made for Ulster, he was emphatic in his reply:

> On the part of Ulster and every loyal man in that province, I repudiate that suggestion. We are prepared and determined to stand and fall, for weal or woe, with every loyal man that lives in Ireland.

From this resolve he never swerved; but Ulster Protestants in general came, later on, to take a more selfish, or more realistic, view of the situation. Saunderson, despite his Ulster birth and Scottish extraction, was essentially Anglo-Irish in his outlook. Though his aggressive Protestantism, and his frequent attacks on what he assumed to be the policy of the Roman Catholic church, were received with acclamation by his followers in Ulster, he always regarded himself as first and foremost an Irishman, with a responsibility for the whole country. He was a devout and active, if somewhat insubordinate, member of the Church of Ireland; and his regular participation in ecclesiastical affairs as a member of the General Synod made him sympathetically aware of the difficulties facing the Protestant minority in the south and west. But his opposition to Home Rule was not based solely on the belief that it would be dangerous to

Protestantism; he was equally convinced that it would ruin the Irish economy, and his concern for the welfare of Ireland was deep-seated and genuine. His County Armagh constituents found some difficulty in understanding his willingness to co-operate, as he occasionally did, with Home Rule members in seeking some advantage for Ireland. But Saunderson, though he had at first been reluctant to consort with men whom he habitually described as 'murderers', made no apology. 'I found myself,' he said, 'with great satisfaction, to be entirely of one mind with my Nationalist opponents'; and together they persuaded the government to extend to Irish farmers a rating subsidy that had already been granted to farmers in Great Britain. The bishop who preached his funeral sermon came nearer the truth than is common on such occasions when he said that Saunderson's convictions arose from 'the passionate belief, which was part of his very soul, that he was fighting for the prosperity, happiness and peace of the land of his birth—the land he loved best on earth'. And that land was the whole island of Ireland, not just the province of Ulster.

But when Saunderson died in 1906 the political climate was already changing. The sweeping Liberal victory in the general election of that year aroused expectations that the policy of Home Rule would soon be revived; and as the threat grew the distinctive character of Ulster Unionism became more strongly marked. When it was proposed during the debate on the Home Rule bill of 1912 that part of the province should be excluded from the authority of the parliament to be set up in Dublin, Saunderson's indignant rejection of the idea was not repeated. Instead, Ulster Unionists took it seriously; and their leader at Westminster, Sir Edward Carson, formally moved the exclusion of the whole of Ulster. The northern Protestants seemed determined to protect themselves, even at the expense of sacrificing their fellow-Protestants in the other three provinces.

Carson's rôle in this transaction must seem, at first sight, a surprising one. He was not an Ulsterman, but a Dubliner, born into a typical middle-class Anglo-Irish family; his father was an architect, practising in Dublin; his mother was the descendant of a Cromwellian planter; two of his uncles were Church of Ireland clergymen. He had been educated at Trinity College, Dublin, the very embodiment of Anglo-Irish culture; and he was one of the university's two representatives at Westminster. It was natural enough that the Irish Unionist M.P.s should have chosen him as their leader, for he was by far the ablest man among them; and, since almost all these M.P.s sat for Ulster constituencies, it was natural also that this leadership should carry with it a dominant position in the Ulster

Unionist movement. But why, one must ask, was Carson, of all men, willing to split the Unionist cause, to make special terms for the north and leave his friends in the south, including his own constituents, to fend for themselves? The answer is that he did not foresee any such result. He was convinced that Home Rule without Ulster would not be viable; and he was convinced also that the Home Rule party would never accept any settlement from which Ulster was excluded. If, then, he could demonstrate, beyond the possibility of doubt, that Ulster would never submit to be governed by a Dublin parliament, the whole policy of Home Rule would have to be abandoned. And to force the abandonment of Home Rule was his governing motive; the special position that he claimed for Ulster was an argument, not an end in itself.

Carson misjudged the situation. The intransigence of Ulster did not, as he had confidently expected, make Irish self-government impossible; instead, the modest proposals of 1912 were replaced, ten years later, by a settlement under which an Irish Free State enjoyed, in practice, sovereign independence. The Ulster Unionists, concerned only with their own local interests, could regard this settlement as a victory, for it left them in control of the six counties within which they could count on a safe majority. But for Carson it was a defeat. He, after all, was an Irishman, not an Ulsterman, and he cared passionately for his country. 'I am resolved to take whatever course is best for Ireland,' he had declared in 1896, when he rejected the Conservative whip because he disagreed with the party's Irish policy. And he had no doubt at all that the best course for Ireland was to remain within the United Kingdom. Like Burke, he believed that the separation of Ireland from England would be ruinous both for Ireland and the Empire; and, like Burke, he advocated the conciliation of the Catholics; he alone, among the Irish Unionist M.P.s, supported the claim of the Roman Catholic bishops for a university that conformed to their principles. Today, Carson is remembered as the champion of Ulster Protestant separatism; but this was not the cause he had at heart, and its success involved the ruin of his true purpose, the preservation of Ireland's position within the United Kingdom. It was, perhaps, a purpose already out of date, and history has dealt hardly with those who followed it. But Carson, though utterly opposed to the end at which the majority of his fellow-countrymen so ardently aimed, sought always what he believed to be the best interests of Ireland. Even if his judgement was at fault his honesty, his courage and his devotion stand beyond question. He was the last of the Anglo-Irish whom circumstances allowed to play a decisive part in the politics of his country; he played and lost, and his defeat marked the end of a political tradition that stretched back over more than seven centuries.

In 1912 it had seemed that the passage of a Home Rule bill was only a matter of time. The House of Lords was against it; but by the terms of the Parliament Act of 1911 the Lords could do no more than delay it for two years. By 1914 Home Rule would be the law of the land, despite the opposition of the Lords. The expected crisis was averted by the outbreak of the Great War in August 1914. Though the Home Rule bill was passed, it was at once suspended until the return of peace; and some optimists hoped that during the interval tension in Ireland would be relaxed to the point at which an amicable settlement could be arranged. But the whole situation was transformed by the insurrection of 1916. In the long run, the insurrection was to make inevitable what was in any case likely, the partition of Ireland; but its more immediate effect was to discredit the policy of Home Rule and stimulate a demand for total separation from Great Britain. In this new situation, the government decided that the search for a settlement could no longer be postponed. Something must be done to satisfy opinion in Ireland and, what was hardly less important, to satisfy the American-Irish, whose anti-British propaganda in the United States was a serious embarrassment to the Allies. But the government, though professing its readiness to act, had no policy to offer; and the best it could do was to assemble, in July 1917, an Irish Convention representing a wide variety of interests, in the vague hope that a group of Irishmen, left to themselves, might work out a settlement satisfactory to all. At this Convention the Anglo-Irish were to appear, for the last time, as a community with a right to share in deciding the destiny of their country.

(4)

The most surprising thing about the Convention of 1917–18 is not its failure—seen in retrospect it must appear an almost hopeless venture from the beginning—but the leading part played in its deliberations by the Anglo-Irish. By this time the two wings of Irish Unionism had become distinct: the Ulster Unionists and the southern Unionists—that is, the Anglo-Irish—were separately represented. Though the latter were not, in point of numbers, altogether negligible, for they amounted to more than 300,000 all told, they lacked the popular basis of either the Ulster Unionists or the Home Rulers. Yet it was they who did most to hold the Convention together, to give its discussions some direction and to set out a basis upon which, in more favourable conditions, a settlement might have been reached.

Their influence owed something to their traditional prestige, and something, also, to the fact that their friends the Conservatives were once more in office, in a coalition government: any proposals that might be put forward would require parliamentary approval, which would be more readily obtained if they had the backing of the Anglo-Irish. Besides this, they occupied a kind of middle position between the Ulster Unionists, on the one hand, and the Home Rulers, on the other, and could act, or try to act, as mediators between the two. But all this would have counted for very little had not their representatives in the Convention been men of ability, clear-sightedness and courage. Of these representatives two were outstanding, Lord Midleton and Archbishop Bernard. Midleton belonged to that small but important group of Anglo-Irish aristocrats who often felt more at home in England than in Ireland, but who none the less had a genuine concern for the country of their ancestors. The first of the family to settle in Ireland, St. John Brodrick, acquired a large estate in County Cork during the Cromwellian period; and the family subsequently played a prominent part in Irish politics. Midleton himself, though born and educated in England, never forgot his family's responsibility towards Ireland; and from his entry into the House of Commons, in 1880, he divided his attention, in typical Anglo-Irish fashion, between Ireland and the Empire. But with the crisis created by the Home Rule bill of 1912 Ireland became his predominant interest, to which he steadily devoted himself during the next ten years. Midleton can hardly be regarded as a typical Anglo-Irishman. His mind was more flexible and his perception of political realities sharper than was common among the Anglo-Irish in general, with whom, indeed, he was sometimes impatient and sometimes out of touch. But his view of Ireland's place in relation to Britain and the Empire was in principle the same as theirs; it was only that he was quicker than they to grasp the difference between what was ideally desirable and what might, in practice, be obtainable.

Bernard was, in background and upbringing, a much more typical representative of the Anglo-Irish community, though in intellectual ability he stood above all but a handful of his contemporaries. The Bernards, like the Brodricks, had been settled in Ireland, in County Kerry, since the seventeenth century; but they were not people of wealth or influence. The archbishop's grandfather started life, in 1808, as a naval surgeon, a position that in those days stood low in the social scale. The surgeon's son, a civil engineer, was employed by the government in India;

and it was in India that John Henry Bernard was born in 1860. A few years later his mother was left a widow, with very small means, and returned to Ireland to bring up her family as best she could. Bernard's early life, though not unhappy, was disciplined by poverty. He entered Trinity College, Dublin, at the early age of fifteen; and, during his undergraduate career and for some years afterwards, he helped to maintain himself by teaching. It was not until he obtained a fellowship, at the age of twenty-four, that he had even a modest degree of financial security. Thereafter, his career ran smoothly. He took orders, and was appointed to a lectureship in the divinity school. His reputation as a scholar grew, not only in Ireland but abroad. Then came promotion, first to the deanery of St. Patrick's, then to the bishopric of Ossory and, in 1915, to the archbishopric of Dublin. It was as a spokesman for the Church of Ireland that Bernard, along with the archbishop of Armagh, John Baptist Crozier, was appointed to the Convention.

Despite this wide difference in background and experience, Midleton and Bernard had reached very similar views about the Irish situation; and throughout the Convention they worked closely together and between them they guided the policy of the small group representing the southern Unionists. Both were convinced that Unionism, in its traditional form, was now a lost cause, that Irish self-government was inevitable and that it would have to go a good deal beyond the modest scheme embodied in the suspended Home Rule Act of 1914. Their purpose was to save what might still be saved from the wreck of their former policy. Three things in particular they aimed at: to maintain close economic and financial links between Ireland and Great Britain; to establish adequate safeguards for the Protestant minority; and to maintain the unity of the country. During the long months that the Convention lasted they pursued these ends with skill, pertinacity and patience; and, after long negotiation with other groups, they were able to embody them in a scheme of self-government that had, or appeared to have, the support of the Home Rule delegates and the acquiescence, at least, of most of the Ulster Unionists. This remarkable achievement owed something to circumstances. The insurrection of 1916 and its aftermath had disturbed the balance of Irish politics. Sinn Féin, which proclaimed the need for total separation from England and which had refused to take part in the Convention, was rapidly coming to dominate Nationalist Ireland. Nothing, now, could save the Home Rule party from destruction but a quick settlement; and its leaders were disposed to snatch at any chance. The Ulster Unionists, with their eyes on the Empire as well as on Ireland, and alarmed at the military situation in Europe, were for the moment in a somewhat less intractable mood than usual. Midleton and Bernard, supported by their colleagues, made skilful use of the opportunity. Both had considerable experience of negotiation—Midleton as a cabinet minister; Bernard in the more restricted but no less arduous field of ecclesiastical politics. But mere skill in dealing with people is not enough to account for the measure of success they attained. What gave the Anglo-Irish their weight in the Convention was the fact that, at a time of doubt and anxiety, they alone were able to take a broad and generous view of the situation and embody it in a coherent plan. They saw clearly that the essential choice before Ireland was that between unity and division. If Sinn Féin were, as seemed likely, to supersede the Home Rule party, then its narrow nationalism and dogmatic commitment to total separation from Great Britain would make any understanding with Ulster Unionism impossible; and Ireland would be plunged into a civil war from which there could be no escape except by the partition of the country. The Anglo-Irish had, of course, a direct interest in averting partition, which would leave the Protestant minority in the south and west hopelessly isolated. But their concern for unity arose from a genuine national feeling, which impressed the Home Rulers and was not without its effect even on the Ulstermen. For a brief space they stood as pointers to an Irish future in which Catholics and Protestants would be united in a common loyalty.

Midleton later claimed that if the scheme had been put to the Convention at the right time it would have been carried easily and that the opportunity was lost through unnecessary delay. This may be an over-optimistic view; but there certainly was a period of delay, during which the apparent unity of purpose crumbled and opposition grew on both wings. When at last the scheme was put to the vote the Ulster Unionists joined forces with the more intransigent Home Rulers, led by three Roman Catholic bishops, to oppose it; and, though it was actually carried by a tiny majority, the opposition was so powerful and so wide-ranging that the scheme could not possibly be regarded as a satisfactory basis for legislation. The Convention was dissolved; and a settlement appeared to be farther off than ever.

The failure of the Convention seemed to justify the refusal of Sinn Féin to take part, and its prestige continued to rise, while the credit of the Home Rule party sank still lower. The funeral of its leader, John Redmond, who died in March 1918 during a visit to London, provided a striking indication of the party's eclipse. In Ireland, the progress of nationalism has been more clearly marked by great funerals than by great battles or great acts of state; and if Redmond had died a few years earlier he would have received a funeral worthy of an emperor. As it was, the arrival of his body in Dublin was hardly noticed except by the few directly concerned; and it was deposited for the night in an obscure chapel before being taken to his native Wexford for burial. One bishop refused even to allow in his cathedral a requiem mass for the soul of the dead leader. All this was significant of a change in ecclesiastical policy: the Home Rule party, so long the faithful ally of the church, had ceased to be useful; and the way must be kept open for an understanding with the rising power of Sinn Féin.

Ireland now moved steadily towards civil war. Even before the end of the Convention the Ulster Unionists had resumed their former entrenched position; and they, like Sinn Féin, were implacably determined to achieve their ends, at whatever cost to the country or themselves. In a situation where differences were to be settled by armed force the Anglo-Irish were helpless; and their intrinsic weakness was increased even further by division among themselves. The willingness of their delegates in the Convention to accept the principle of self-government for Ireland aroused a strong reaction among those who still believed that the parliamentary union could be preserved intact; and for the next few years, until the settlement of 1921–2 made further activity meaningless, the Anglo-Irish were divided into those who supported and those who opposed Midleton's policy of compromise. These years were a period of immense suffering for the scattered and helpless Protestant minority in the south and west. The bitter experience through which they passed, though commonly forgotten or ignored, is yet of historical importance; for it was one cause, even if a relatively minor one, of that catastrophic decline in the Protestant population of the area that has been such a marked feature of Irish life since the establishment of self-government.

The Anglo-Irish themselves can hardly have expected this development when, in the last stages of the conflict, they returned briefly to the political scene and helped to prepare the way for a settlement. By the summer of 1921 the struggle between the Crown forces and the Irish Republican Army, the military wing of Sinn Féin, had reached a stage at which it seemed impossible that either could gain a decisive victory; and political leaders on both sides were willing to negotiate, if some means could be found of bringing them together. A small group of Anglo-Irishmen headed by Midleton, accepted the task; and, taking in their hands not only their lives but their reputations, they established direct contact with De Valera. It was through their mediation that a truce was arranged and the negotiations that led eventually to the Treaty of December 1921 begun. In bringing the two sides together, they apparently considered it unnecessary to ask for any prior assurance that the special interests of the Anglo-Irish would be considered in whatever settlement might emerge. Whether such an assurance would have been given must be doubtful; but without it their position was certainly hopeless. The British government, glad to get out of an impossible situation on any tolerable terms, was willing to leave the Protestant minority to its fate; and there was no reason why the negotiators on the other side should spontaneously offer concessions to a small and politically powerless group which they had long regarded as part of the 'English garrison'. Besides this, the men who were about to take over the government of the greater part of Ireland were committed to the building up of a Catholic and Gaelic state. They were certainly prepared to extend formal toleration to those who differed from them, but only so far as this did not prevent the realization of their ideal. Within a few years, though there was little change in the law, there had come about a marked change in what might be called the tone of government and of society in general. An Anglo-Irish Protestant, looking at the Ireland in which he now found himself, might well have said with Garibaldi, 'They have made me a stranger in the land of my birth.'

VII

The Tradition in Literature

---

(1)

'English', said Bernard Shaw, 'is the native language of Irishmen.' This was certainly true when he said it; and all the effort and all the money that have been devoted to the revival of Gaelic during the past fifty years have hardly altered the situation. But when the Anglo-Irish first established their ascendancy, two centuries before Shaw's birth, Gaelic was still the everyday language of a very large section of the population, perhaps even of a majority; and over much of the country it maintained its position until the Great Famine of the 1840s transformed rural society. Yet even during this period English was the dominant language, the language of government and commerce, of books and newspapers, the language through which Ireland was known to the outside world. Gaelic Ireland had its poets and story-tellers, who found their public among the peasantry with whom they lived. Occasionally, they had patrons among the upper classes, some of whom knew enough Gaelic to understand and translate their work. But it was not until the romantic nationalism of the nineteenth century brought with it a new interest in Gaelic culture that they acquired a wider fame; and, even then, it was mainly in English translations that their works were known to the general public. To most people in Ireland as well as in the world outside 'Irish literature' still meant the writings of authors who wrote in English. And from the seventeenth century to the twentieth most of these authors belonged to that Anglo-Irish tradition with which we are here concerned. There is no exaggeration in Yeats's proud claim for the Protestants of Ireland: 'We have created most of the modern literature of this country.'

The literature to which Yeats referred was not in any sense exclusively 'Irish'. The eighteenth-century writers whom he admired—Swift, Berkeley, Burke and Goldsmith—have their place in the general corpus of English literature; and the same may be said of their contemporaries and successors, including Yeats himself. Ireland lies so close to England and is so much exposed to English economic and social influences that Irish writers using the English language have been unable to establish an independent literature of their own. It is true that since the later nineteenth century the term 'Anglo-Irish literature' has had some currency; but it is a term without any precise and accurate meaning. Originally, it was used to describe the work of a group of writers, including Yeats and Synge, who sought inspiration in Irish themes; and here it is at least understandable, though the work of these writers can hardly be regarded as constituting a distinct 'literature': at most, they formed a local school within the confines of English literature in general. Later on, the term acquired a more extended application; and, if one is to judge by the contexts in which it occurs, came to mean the whole body of work by Irish-born writers who used the English language. In this sense, it can serve no useful purpose and may be dangerously misleading. The authors thus lumped together are not distinguished from their English contemporaries by any common characteristic beyond the mere fact of their having been born in Ireland; and their work as a whole, taken out of its proper place in the main stream of English literature, displays none of those elements of coherence or continuity that would entitle it to be regarded as a distinct and independent literature, or to be described in national or quasi-national terms.

This misuse of the term 'Anglo-Irish' must not be allowed to obscure or diminish the literary achievement of the Anglo-Irish properly so called— that section of the population of Ireland whose tradition we are here tracing. It is upon their work that the literary reputation of Ireland very largely depends. Yet they never thought of literature in merely national terms; even when they were striving to promote an Irish cause they remained conscious of a wider relationship and a wider responsibility and refused to confine themselves within a narrower world than that to which their cultural inheritance gave them the entry. We see here an expression of the ambivalence that seemed inseparable from their condition: like their medieval predecessors, they were 'the English of Ireland', a people whose total allegiance could never be given to a single community; and not even political hostility could destroy their sense of kinship with those who spoke the same tongue.

This ambivalence helps to explain a seemingly paradoxical change of literary fashion among the Anglo-Irish. In the eighteenth century, when they confidently regarded themselves as the representatives of a distinct nation and firmly asserted the constitutional rights of Ireland, Anglo-Irish authors rarely wrote on Irish topics except on those directly concerned with matters of political, religious or economic controversy. Though some of them maintained a scholarly interest in Irish antiquities and in the

Gaelic language, attempts to use this material for imaginative literature were few and feeble. When Henry Flood, patriot though he was and a patron of Gaelic studies, wished to provide his protégé, Thomas Dermody, with a subject on which to write, he did not put forward any Irish theme but suggested a poem on 'The development of the British constitution'. Yet after the parliamentary union, when the Anglo-Irish, as a body, quickly abandoned any idea of a separate political nationality, they began to develop, for the first time, a sense of national responsibility in literature and to seek for literary themes in the history, the society and the scenery of their own country. Their Kingdom of Ireland had disappeared; they had readily transferred their allegiance from Dublin to Westminster; but they could not forget that they were Irishmen, and their sense of being Irish, which they could no longer express in political terms, found an outlet in literature.

This change was not so sudden as might at first sight appear; and it certainly owed a good deal to the Romantic movement that was affecting the whole of Western Europe at this period. But it does reflect in a very clear way the situation and outlook of the Anglo-Irish. While their national identity was protected by the terms of the constitution they were content to merge their literary life in that of England. When this protection was removed, when they could no longer express their nationality in political terms and, indeed, no longer wished to do so, they must show that Ireland had a distinctive contribution to make to the literature of the English language. Their efforts to achieve this end provide the starting point for almost all the significant writing that has since come out of Ireland.

(2)

The parliamentary union marks, at least approximately, a line of division between two phases in the literary outlook of the Anglo-Irish. It also suggests a double answer to the question with which we are here concerned: In what ways did the tradition of the Anglo-Irish find expression in literature? Some of them, particularly in the post-union period, display their Anglo-Irish character openly and consciously in their choice of themes and their mode of handling them. With others, including most of those of the eighteenth century as well as some of later date, such explicit indications of their background are either incidental or altogether lacking. Sometimes, indeed, their work is indistinguishable from that of their English-born contemporaries; but sometimes, also, it reveals a cast of mind that is characteristically Anglo-Irish, even though the subject-matter is neutral.

It is thus possible to trace the Anglo-Irish tradition in literature along two lines. One line runs through the work of those authors who found in Irish life material for creative writing; the other through the work of those authors who reveal characteristically Anglo-Irish qualities, even though their subject-matter has no explicit relationship to Ireland. This second line is often obscure and sometimes broken; but it reappears at intervals and stretches from Swift to Bernard Shaw.

The interest in Irish themes that became a marked feature of Anglo-Irish literary life in the generation after the union can be traced back to the eighteenth century and has one of its most important sources in the work and influence of Henry Brooke. He was born about 1703, the son of a clergyman and small landowner, and passed most of his life in Ireland, devoting himself to literary pursuits, which brought him some financial return and a considerable reputation. But the works on which his reputation rested and by which he is still remembered—in reference-books if not among readers—are not on Irish themes and they were intended primarily for an English public. His best-known play, *Gustavus Vasa*, deals with the career of a Swedish national hero. His long poem, *Universal Beauty*, is on an abstract subject. His novel, *The Fool of Quality*, depicts aristocratic life in England. But Brooke also showed a genuine, though somewhat inactive, interest in the history and culture of his native land. He projected works on Irish history and Irish mythology; but in neither case did he get beyond the publication of a prospectus. He talked about learning Gaelic, but never did so. He began a long poem in blank verse based on the legendary history of Ulster's heroic age; but he left it unfinished. All this amounted to very little; but Brooke redeemed his own lack of perseverance by imparting his interest in Gaelic literature to his daughter, Charlotte. She, more determined than her father, learned the language; and she spent much of her time in collecting Gaelic songs and poems current in oral tradition. Some of these she turned into English verse; and in 1789 she published a volume containing both the originals and her own translations, with the title *Reliques of Irish Poetry*. The process of collecting, translating and publishing Gaelic verse, which has gone on ever since, thus finds one of its earliest sources in the enterprise of a family that was, in background and status, typical of the Anglo-Irish middle class.

The Brookes were not, however, alone in their desire to promote the study of Gaelic literature. Charlotte was encouraged in her work by

Joseph Cooper Walker, a wealthy dilettante whose wide-ranging interests included Irish antiquities; and the fact that her *Reliques of Irish Poetry* was published in Dublin indicates that there was a local market for such works. But there is little to suggest that among the Anglo-Irish in general there was at this time any demand for literature with a national flavour. The reading public was not large; but the theatre was very popular, in the provinces as well as in Dublin; and the drama probably provides the best guide to prevailing literary taste. Plays with an Irish setting were very few indeed; and of the few only one can be regarded as a genuine attempt to depict the Irish society of the period—Charles Macklin's *True-born Irishman*. Apart from two or three wooden and unsuccessful attempts at historical drama, the rest were mere farces, of which the most popular was Thomas Sheridan's *Captain O'Blunder*. Irish audiences wanted to see the plays that London was talking about; and Irish dramatists, with their eyes on the London stage, naturally chose themes that would be acceptable in England.

The parliamentary union did not bring about an immediate change in these attitudes. But the Anglo-Irish, as they adjusted themselves to the new situation, were uncomfortably aware that their country and its capital might soon become little more than a provincial backwater. This feeling was strongest among the middle classes, which had always been the backbone of the Anglo-Irish tradition. The nobility and the greater landowners were, generally speaking, as much at home in England as in Ireland; but for the minor gentry, the professional classes, the bankers and the well-to-do merchants, Dublin was the centre of social and intellectual life. They saw no reason why its prestige should be allowed to vanish because it was no longer the capital of a distinct kingdom. It had ceased to be the meeting-place of a parliament; but it could still be a meeting-place for those interested in literature and scholarship. A determination to assert and strengthen Dublin's position in this respect lay behind the repeated attempts, during the first generation after the union, to establish in the city something that Ireland had hitherto lacked, a literary periodical of high quality. The task proved a difficult one; but at last, in 1833, the *Dublin University Magazine* began its long and distinguished career.

In origin and outlook the *Dublin University Magazine* was a typical expression of the Anglo-Irish spirit as it had developed since the union. It was founded by a group of young men in Trinity College, including Isaac Butt, who soon became editor; and its connection with the College, though never official, remained close. Its political character became less strongly marked as time went on; but to begin with it was aggressively Tory and Protestant. At a time when Catholic Emancipation was only a few years old, when the Tories had hardly recovered their breath after the shattering blow of the First Reform Act, when Ireland was in the grip of a 'tithe war', when parliament was on the point of curtailing the Irish ecclesiastical establishment by the suppression of ten bishoprics, the magazine came forward as an uncompromising defender of the Church of Ireland and of her indefeasible right to tithe. Not content with a defensive rôle, it carried the war into the enemy's territory. An early number contains a review of Thomas Moore's *Irish Gentleman in Search of a Religion*, a review in which Moore's not very profound apologia is made an excuse for an unrestrained attack on popery and all its works. Yet along with its firm assertion of Protestant ascendancy the magazine also advocated what can best be described as a policy of literary nationalism. It encouraged Irish authors to write on Irish subjects; it devoted its reviews largely, though by no means exclusively, to works of Irish interest; it did what it could to promote the publication of Irish works in Ireland rather than in England—the first number noted with satisfaction that William Carleton's *Traits and Stories of the Irish Peasantry*, which had appeared in book form the previous year, had been published in Dublin and hailed this as a good omen for the future.

This interest in Carleton reflects the magazine's concern about the quality of Irish fiction. It set itself to train the reading public to distinguish between true and false representations of Irish life; and, in particular, it protested against the absurd travesties that were often accepted as typically 'Irish'. Such training was not uncalled for, at least among English readers. The imaginary titles that Thackeray cites in *Pendennis*—'the comic Irish novel of Barney Brallaghan', 'the rollicking Hibernian story of Looney MacTwolter'—are hardly more fantastic than the titles of works actually published. Against this kind of misrepresentation the *Dublin University Magazine* maintained, by precept and example, that Irish themes could provide material for serious fiction and that it was the duty of Irish authors to treat such themes faithfully, with humour where humour was appropriate, but without any playing to the English gallery.

The counsel given by the *Dublin University Magazine* was not made unnecessary by the fact that two novelists of considerable power, Maria Edgeworth and Lady Morgan, had already shown how Irish themes could be effectively handled in fiction. Maria Edgeworth led the way with *Castle Rackrent*, published in 1801, followed by *The Absentee* in 1812 and *Ormond* in 1817. Lady Morgan later claimed that her *Wild Irish Girl* had been the first novel of Irish life; but her statements about her own career are rarely reliable, and the *Wild Irish Girl* did not, in fact, appear until 1806. But, although it has not worn so well as *Castle Rackrent*, it was more widely popular at the time and ran through seven editions in less than two years. Lady Morgan's later output, which was large and varied, included three more Irish novels: *O'Donnel*, in 1814; *Florence McCarthy*, in 1816; *The O'Briens and the O'Flahertys*, in 1827. But none of these attained the same degree of popular success as the *Wild Irish Girl*.

Both these authors looked at Irish society from a point of view very different from Carleton's. Miss Edgeworth's long residence in County Longford, where she assisted her father in the management of his estate, made her familiar with the countryside and its people, among whom she was a frequent and welcome visitor. Yet, despite these advantages, it was impossible for her to know peasant life from the inside. She described it with sympathy and understanding, but also with a detachment that was not wholly free from a sense of superiority. Lady Morgan, Sydney Owenson before her marriage, came from a very different background. Her father was the son of poor parents in County Mayo, whose family name of MacOwen he later anglicized. He made his way to England, went on the stage and had considerable success both in London and Dublin. His daughter tried to make out that the MacOwens, despite their poverty, were gentry by origin, and she asserted that her paternal grandfather had made a romantic runaway match with the daughter of a neighbouring landlord. Whatever the truth or falsehood of these claims, she herself was brought up in the mixed and shifting world of the theatre; and her rise in life was due to her own abilities and not to family connections. The most one can say is that her father's Protestantism, which may possibly be an indication of social status, undoubtedly eased her progress. Her vivacity and her talents soon attracted notice; she found patrons among the aristocracy; and in 1812 she married Sir Thomas Morgan, an eminent English surgeon practising in Dublin. From this time onwards, until her death in 1859, she moved freely in the fashionable society of Dublin and London. In politics she was strongly liberal. She supported Catholic Emancipation; and her Irish novels are marked by a nationalism that is wholly absent from Miss Edgeworth's. Despite her ancestry, she knew little of the Irish countryside and still less of the life of the peasantry. Her romantic picture of an aristocratic Gaelic tradition surviving after centuries of Saxon rule was the product of a lively imagination undisciplined by any careful attention to the actual state of affairs.

Miss Edgeworth and Lady Morgan, despite their widely differing backgrounds, both belong to the Anglo-Irish tradition. Carleton, the son of a Roman Catholic peasant family and originally intended for the priesthood, clearly does not. But it was Anglo-Irish influence that started him on his career as an author. His *Traits and Stories of the Irish Peasantry*, published in book form in 1832, had originally appeared in the *Christian Examiner*, a Church of Ireland periodical founded in 1825 by Caesar Otway, himself a writer of some distinction; and much of Carleton's later work appeared in the *Dublin University Magazine*. It is true that Otway was originally attracted by Carleton's outspoken comments on the religious life of the peasantry, which he hoped might be of service to the Protestant cause. But the support that Carleton continued to receive among the Anglo-Irish had its root in genuine literary interest. He could describe vividly and faithfully, and from first-hand experience, a large section of Irish life that they themselves could see only from the outside.

Almost at the same time as Carleton there appeared three other Roman Catholic novelists: the brothers John and Michael Banim and Gerald Griffin. Like him, they found their themes in rural life; and they too were encouraged by the *Dublin University Magazine*, where some of their work was published. But it was a long time before any successor of comparable ability appeared. The continued popularity of Charles Kickham's *Knocknagow*, published in 1879, is not so much a tribute to the literary merits of the book, which are negligible, as an indication of the fact that Catholic Ireland failed to produce, at this period, any novelist of real power. Kickham certainly understood the outlook of the Irish peasantry better than, say, Charles Lever or Samuel Lover; but he lacked the inventive genius and the command of language to give independent life to his work. The truth is that throughout the nineteenth century the task of representing the life of Ireland in fiction was left almost entirely to writers of the Anglo-Irish tradition. None of them stands in the front rank of novelists. But a century that saw the publication of *Castle Rackrent* in its first decade and *The Real Charlotte* in its last has some claim to distinction.

In encouraging the writing of novels and stories of Irish life the *Dublin University Magazine* played an important part. Samuel Lover was one of its founders, Charles Lever was for a time its editor, and both were among its contributors; some of Lever's best-known novels, including *Harry Lorrequer*, *Charles O'Malley* and *Jack Hinton*, appeared in it as serials before being published in book form. But the magazine was equally concerned to promote the study of Gaelic literature and its translation into English. In this task no one took a more important share than Sir Samuel Ferguson. Despite his Scottish ancestry Ferguson was easily absorbed into the Anglo-Irish community. Though he was born in Belfast and received his early education there, he spent most of his life in Dublin and he was, by assimilation if not by ancestry, a typical member of the Anglo-Irish professional middle class. He made his literary début in 1832, with a poem, 'The Forging of the Anchor', in *Blackwood's Magazine*, in which he continued to write for some years. But he had a strong sense of duty to Ireland and he had ideas that he wished to spread among Irish readers. From the time the *Dublin University Magazine* was founded, in 1833, he was one of its most frequent and most influential contributors in the field of Irish studies. He set himself to stimulate, especially among Protestants, an interest in the history and antiquities of Ireland, partly as a means of establishing better understanding between Irishmen of different faiths and different politics, but mainly because he saw in them the basis for a distinctively Irish contribution to literature. Again and again, in books and articles, he comes back to this theme. 'The Protestant wealth and intelligence of the country' must, he asserts, 'cultivate an acquaintance with its ancient literature and traditions'. He compares the history of ancient Ireland with the history of ancient Greece and urges Irishmen to cherish their traditions as 'the seeds of a new literature'.

Ferguson laboured hard to put his principles into practice; and some of his translations, though they have been criticized by scholars, are poems of real power and beauty. But his attempts to familiarize a wide circle of readers with the history of Ireland, and especially of ancient Ireland, were much less successful. Neither the *Hibernian Nights' Entertainments* nor the *Lays of the Western Gael* achieved the sort of circulation for which he had hoped. His long narrative poems, *Congal* and *Conary*, were well received by the critics; but they made little lasting impression on the general public. Ferguson's enthusiasm was widely recognized. People of all classes and all opinions applauded his patriotism. But the literary revolution that he set out to achieve was beyond his powers. And yet, indirectly, he accomplished much more than was apparent in his lifetime; for among those who felt his influence most keenly was the young William Butler Yeats, who was destined to become the greatest of Anglo-Irish poets. The very exaggeration of Yeats's tribute to Ferguson's work shows how deeply it had moved him:

The author of these poems is the greatest poet Ireland has produced, because the most central and most Celtic. Whatever the future may bring forth in the way of a truly great and national literature . . . will find its morning in these three volumes of one who was made by the purifying flame of national sentiment the one man of his time who wrote heroic poetry—one who, among the somewhat sybaritic singers of his day, was like some aged sea-king sitting among the inland wheat and poppies—the savour of the sea about him, and its strength.

It was through Ferguson, and especially through his influence on Yeats, that the spirit of the *Dublin University Magazine*, which had ceased publication in 1877, survived into the closing decades of the nineteenth century to inspire a new literary movement; and, once again, it was the Anglo-Irish who played a dominant rôle. Those who gave the movement importance at the time and by whose works and names it is still remembered all belonged, by birth and inheritance if not by conviction, to the Church of Ireland: Yeats himself, Standish James O'Grady, J. M. Synge, Douglas Hyde, George Russell (A.E.), Lady Gregory. And three of these were directly associated with the movement's most important legacy to later generations: Yeats, Synge and Lady Gregory were the original directors of the Abbey Theatre.

This new movement, commonly spoken of as the Irish Literary Revival, was more broadly based than the earlier movement that had led to the founding of the *Dublin University Magazine* in the 1830s. It had no tinge of the aggressive Protestant Toryism that had marked the magazine in its early years, and it was, in fact, free from any political commitment. Its aims were national, but not nationalist; and it had room for men of widely differing views. O'Grady, whose *History of Ireland*, succeeding where Ferguson had failed, had made the legendary heroes of ancient Ireland familiar to the popular mind, was a convinced and active Unionist. Yeats felt a romantic attachment to the Fenian and republican tradition. Russell, though not unsympathetic to nationalist aspirations, feared that separation from Britain would mean the ruin of the Irish economy. Hyde professed to stand apart from politics; but he was, in one way at least, more revolutionary than any of the rest, for his declared aim was to establish Gaelic as the national language, or, as he put it himself, to 'de-Anglicize' Ireland. But, whatever their differences, all were convinced that literature had a vital part to play in the national life and that it was their responsibility to show how this could be done.

In the circumstances, it was natural that they should feel obliged to choose Irish themes; and in practice they confined themselves even more narrowly. The romanticism that was already dying elsewhere in Western

Europe still survived in Ireland; and it influenced, one might almost say dictated, both their choice of material and the use they made of it. For the most part, their poems, plays and stories either deal with myth and legend or present a picture of peasant society that is hardly nearer to the realities of everyday life as it was lived in the Ireland of the time. To say this is not to belittle their work; there have been few richer periods in the literary history of Ireland. But the function of a 'national literature', which is what they set out to create, is to interpret a nation to itself and to the world; and if we turn to the works of the authors associated with the Literary Revival the interpretation of Ireland and Irish life that we find there is only a small and unrepresentative fraction of the total Irish experience; and the effectiveness of what we do find is sometimes weakened by an air of artificiality and make-believe.

One might say, indeed, that something of this incompleteness appears in the works of all Anglo-Irish authors who have found their material in the life of Ireland, though not all of them are guilty of artificiality. The cause lay less in themselves than in their background. In their relations with the great majority of their fellow-countrymen they could never effectively bridge the gap created by difference of religion and all that that implies in Irish society. Try as they might, they remained spectators rather than participants in much of what was of vital importance to the Roman Catholic population. They had inherited a distinctive tradition; and they must accept its limitations along with its advantages.

The effect of this distinctiveness appears most clearly in the novelists. In Lady Morgan its presence is all the more striking because she herself would have wished to disown it. She used her novels to counter Protestant and English prejudice against the Irish Roman Catholics and to promote the cause of Emancipation. Yet, even in doing so, she takes up the position of an advocate speaking on behalf of his clients rather than that of a representative speaking on behalf of the people to whom he belongs. Lever, who had no political purpose and wrote only to entertain, came nearer to presenting a balanced picture. He was more closely acquainted with the realities of Irish life and he covered a wider social spectrum. In his pages, rich and poor, townsmen and countrymen, Protestants and Roman Catholics mingle together. The action is sometimes improbable and the characters are sometimes overdrawn; but the total effect is to give a genuine if highly coloured picture of the Ireland of his day. And yet, though Lever is no propagandist, though he shows no obvious prejudice, one is constantly aware that he views the Irish scene from within the Protestant community. His Roman Catholic characters, however favourably and sympathetically treated, still remain in some measure external to him—they remain the friendly Protestant's conception of good and amiable Catholics.

In the novels of Somerville and Ross, more than half a century later, the viewpoint is frankly that of the Protestant landed class. Here, the religious distinction corresponds very closely to distinction of social status; and Roman Catholics inhabit a separate world which is recognized as one that can be known only from without. We see them as they appeared to the Protestants among whom they lived, rather than as they really were. In *The Real Charlotte*, where the social range is extended somewhat, it is extended only within the Protestant community. Charlotte Mullin and Francie Fitzpatrick have an independent life of their own; but there are no Roman Catholic characters of similar rank in society. Even *The Big House of Inver*, where the heroine is herself a Catholic, is hardly an exception to this general rule. Shibby's whole outlook is dominated by her relationship to the Prendevilles, the decadent Protestant landlord family of which she is an illegitimate member; and it is the Big House itself, rather than any human character, that dominates this powerful book.

It is certainly difficult, and perhaps impossible, for an Irish novelist to give a whole picture of a society so deeply divided as that of Ireland. If he is true to his material the division must be reflected in his work; and the manner in which it is reflected is bound to be coloured by his own background. The Anglo-Irish novelists cannot fairly be blamed for giving an incomplete or one-sided view of Irish society. They described Ireland as they saw it; and from Maria Edgeworth down to Somerville and Ross they saw it through the eyes of the Protestant ascendancy. The picture they represented was misleading only because it was not balanced by any companion piece. From the middle of the nineteenth century to the early decades of the twentieth, Catholic Ireland failed to produce any novelist of sufficient ability to catch and keep the attention of the English-speaking world.

The divided state of Irish society had a less direct and less obvious influence on poetry than on fiction. Poetry, indeed, might seem to be a neutral world, in which differing social traditions could mingle freely. But, in fact, the wider a poet's range, the more intense his feeling, the more likely he is to reveal the inner consciousness of the society to which he belongs. Yeats sought inspiration in the Gaelic past of Ireland. He embodied in his poems the legends, the beliefs and the language of the Catholic peasantry of the West. His enthusiasm was stirred by the republican movement and he commemorated the events of 1916 in splendid verse. But he could not escape from the influence of his Anglo-Irish background. His nationalism belonged to the eighteenth century rather than to the nineteenth or twentieth. His sympathy with the peasantry was romantic, not social and political. The Big House, which stood, in the popular mind, for landlord tyranny and alien domination, was to him a symbol of the orderly and aristocratic life that was his ideal. When events forced him to recognize the reality of the religious and cultural cleavage in Ireland there was no doubt on which side he stood. Writing in the *Irish Statesman*, in 1925, he rejected any idea that Roman Catholics were in some way more truly 'Irish' than Protestants, and, speaking in the name of the Protestant community, he called upon the Protestants to assert their distinctive position in the life of the country: 'Ireland is not more theirs than ours. We must glory in our difference, be as proud of it as they are of theirs.'

Yeats's pride in the achievement of Protestant Ireland was expressed in his growing admiration for the eighteenth century—the century of Swift and Berkeley, of Burke and Goldsmith. It is their influence, not that of Gaelic myth and legend, that dominates his later work. He had come, in the end, to the place where he was most naturally at home, the 'great century' of the Anglo-Irish tradition.

(3)

The writers whom we have so far considered found material for their novels, plays or poems in the life of Ireland; and from the way in which they treat Irish themes we can assess, with some confidence, the influence of their Anglo-Irish origins on their work. The same Anglo-Irish influence is also to be found in works where the subject-matter has no obvious connection with Ireland; and here it is, naturally, less open and direct. With some Anglo-Irish writers it is, perhaps, possible to trace the influence of an Irish background in their use of language; but that is irrelevant to the present purpose. Our concern is to see how the characteristic Anglo-Irish qualities, bred in the special circumstances of Ireland, could find expression, sometimes at least, in a writer's outlook on the world and on society in general. The works of three great eighteenth-century authors —Swift, Burke and Goldsmith—show how varied that expression could be.

Both Swift and Burke wrote much on Ireland; and, though they held widely differing views both about the internal affairs of the country and about its relations with England, the attitudes they display are typically

Anglo-Irish. Here, however, we are concerned with their much more extensive writings on other topics. And it is, in fact, these writings that have determined their rank in literature. The *Drapier's Letters* and the *Modest Proposal* certainly stand high among Swift's works; but, even without them, the *Tale of a Tub*, *Gulliver's Travels* and the *Argument against Abolishing Christianity* place him among the greatest writers of English prose. Burke's Irish pamphlets, though historically important, do not approach the heights of the *Reflections on the French Revolution* or the *Letters on a Regicide Peace*. Goldsmith, the third of the trio, never wrote anything on an Irish subject; and references to Ireland, scattered through his works, are few and unimportant. These three, though they differ in so many ways, all reveal in their writings the influence of a common background.

Of the three, it is Swift who embodies most clearly and fully the characteristic Anglo-Irish qualities. There is something of a paradox here, for his family had no roots in Ireland; and he always regarded his Irish birth as an unhappy accident. Throughout life, even while he was defending the rights of Ireland against English oppression, he persisted in regarding England as his 'own country'. But his sensitive nature responded readily to environment; and he became, to adapt an old saying, more Anglo-Irish than the Anglo-Irish themselves. His literary genius would have found expression wherever he had been born; but the form it actually took was strongly marked by the character of the Anglo-Irish community to which, however unwillingly, he belonged.

The most pervasive Anglo-Irish quality is a kind of ambivalence, or ambiguity of outlook, arising from the need to be at once Irish and English, and leading sometimes to detachment, sometimes to a fierce aggressiveness that may, on occasion, mark an underlying sense of insecurity. This ambivalence is one of the most constant and most powerful elements in the work of Swift; and in him it may well have been reinforced by his devotion to the Church of England, which stood poised between popery, on the one hand, and a more radical Protestantism, on the other, in much the same way as the Anglo-Irish stood between the 'mere Irish' and the 'English by birth'. It is Swift's ambivalent position that gives depth to the best of his satirical work. What he is attacking is not something wholly external to himself, but something with which he feels, even while he shrinks from it, an essential and inescapable relationship. What makes the Yahoos so terrifying is not simply that they are ferocious and filthy, but that they are so clearly akin to the kindly and humane Captain Lemuel Gulliver and, through him, to Swift himself and to the reader.

Equally prominent in Swift's work is the arrogance that was bred in Irish Protestants by their sense of superiority to the Roman Catholics, an arrogance that they commonly took with them wherever they went. In Swift it was sometimes exaggerated almost to the point of mania and not infrequently it warped his relations with his fellow-men. Even in his writings one can now and then detect, in his defence of some cause or institution, a sense of personal resentment arising from offended pride. But his arrogance is also a source of strength and it gives his satire a magisterial quality that it would be hard to parallel in the whole range of English literature.

Burke's Irish roots ran deeper than Swift's and his concern about Ireland was more unselfish. But his career, from an early age, was wholly in England and his political thinking was dominated by what he conceived to be the interests of Britain and the Empire. Even so, the influence of background and upbringing survived; and his work reveals, though not so clearly and directly as Swift's, some typically Anglo-Irish attitudes. He had none of Swift's fierce personal pride. He did not thrust himself forward as the equal of the great men of his party; and he was content to be, in a way that Swift could never have stomached, their social and economic dependant. But his admiration of aristocracy and his reverence for authority may be seen as an expression of Anglo-Irish pride in domination translated into institutional terms. And his attitude displays another Anglo-Irish quality, ambivalence. Despite his love of justice and his sympathy with the oppressed, whether Hindu peasants or Irish Catholics, the notion of popular rule was abhorrent to him, as an upsetting of the established order. He would not separate the present from the past; and all that had the sanction of history seemed to him worthy of respect. But at this point he stopped. Though he always insisted on the right conferred by prescription, on the respect due to established institutions and vested interests, he opposed any demand for an investigation into origins, into the foundation on which institutions and interests had arisen. He could defend them as part of the historical development of society; but he would not subject the justice of their origins to the test of historical evidence. It would be rash to assume that this ambiguity in Burke's thinking must necessarily be derived from his Anglo-Irish background. But no line of argument could have been better suited to the position of the Protestant ascendancy, whose constitutional claims rested on a notion of corporate continuity that disguised or ignored revolutionary changes both in population and in the distribution of property. The fact that Burke himself had little sympathy with the men who were most forward in asserting these claims may serve to emphasize the ambivalence of his attitude but cannot affect its appropriateness to the society in which his mind was formed.

In Goldsmith, the characteristic Anglo-Irish pride is softened and subdued by his gentler nature into an observant detachment—a detachment that certainly does not preclude sympathy for others but that does raise the observer above his surroundings. It is, perhaps, in the *Citizen of the World* that this detachment is most clearly apparent; and here it is reinforced by—or, one might say, merged with—a typically Anglo-Irish ambivalence. The book employs a literary device popular at the time—a view of society as seen through the eyes of a fictitious foreign visitor, in this case a Chinese philosopher who is reporting his experiences in England to a friend in Peking. Of the many writers who have employed this device few have handled it so successfully as Goldsmith; and it is hard not to feel that much of his success arose from the fact that he was, in reality as well as in fiction, a visitor. And he was a visitor of a special sort; one whose background and education made it easy for him to sympathize with English ways of thought and to understand English prejudices, while retaining at the same time an inner sense of distinctiveness that enabled him to observe and comment with a clarity and independence that a native could hardly have attained. The very title of the book may, perhaps, indicate that Goldsmith himself had realized this situation. An Anglo-Irishman who feels the tug of conflicting loyalties, who is conscious of standing between two nations and belonging fully to neither, may well be tempted to abandon both and proclaim himself a citizen of the world.

This unconscious revelation of typical Anglo-Irish qualities, exemplified in the work of Swift, Burke and Goldsmith, is much less evident in the Anglo-Irish writers of the nineteenth century. Of those whose names are now remembered the majority chose to write on Irish themes; and it is in their treatment of these themes, rather than in their outlook on the world in general, that the influence of their background can be traced. Among the rest, from George Darley to Oscar Wilde, there is hardly one whose work bears an unmistakable Anglo-Irish imprint. It would almost seem as if the characteristic spirit of the Anglo-Irish could no longer find expression save in writings directly concerned with Ireland. But any such conclusion is effectively negatived by the life and work of one dominant figure, George Bernard Shaw.

Shaw belonged by birth to that middle layer of society from which almost all the major Anglo-Irish writers came. His father was a solicitor turned businessman; his mother was the daughter of a debt-ridden County Carlow landlord; he had connections among the Church of Ireland clergy. But his father's mismanagement kept the family in almost continuous poverty; and Shaw himself began to earn his living before he was sixteen. Five years later, he left Dublin for London; and the rest of his life was passed in England. But the influence of family background and early experience was so strong that he remained an Anglo-Irishman until his death, three-quarters of a century later.

With Shaw, the Anglo-Irish arrogance is, at least in appearance, purely intellectual. He never seems to doubt that the views he puts forward are both important and right; and he directs his sharpest criticism against those who either lack the knowledge they claim to have or are incapable of applying it properly. But the preface to *John Bull's Other Island* suggests very strongly that his arrogance had a more than merely intellectual basis and owed something to the need so often felt by the Anglo-Irish in England to assert their position and to claim the respect that they were sure was due to them. It is harder to find in Shaw the characteristic Anglo-Irish ambivalence, for he was too sure of himself to have any doubt about where he stood. But he does show the detachment that ambivalence often produced in other Anglo-Irish writers. He views English society in the same uncommitted way as Goldsmith, though he has little of the grace or of the gentle tolerance that mark all Goldsmith's work. If he is to be compared with any earlier Anglo-Irish writer it must be with Swift. Like Swift, he had a strong conviction of his own powers; like Swift, he wrote not merely to entertain but to persuade; and his prose style has something of Swift's simple directness. But these resemblances lie on the surface; and Shaw shows little of the urgent sense of purpose that marks so much of Swift's writing and still less of the 'savage indignation' that gives a terrifying strength to his satire.

When Shaw died, in 1950, the Anglo-Irish community, in which he had been brought up, had been in decline for a generation and seemed to be moving towards extinction. Political and social changes had destroyed its influence; and even its will to survive might appear to be fading away. Its literary achievement remains; but the strength and vitality from which that achievement sprang belong to the past, not to the present.

Epilogue

The Anglo-Irish tradition is now more than eight hundred years old; and the conditions from which it sprang are older still. The geographical situation of the British Isles is such that Ireland and Great Britain cannot stand wholly apart: if the Irish Sea forbids a complete union the Atlantic Ocean equally forbids a total separation. Strong links between the two islands existed long before Hervey de Montmorency and his followers landed on the Wexford coast in 1169. It was because of those links that an Irish king had turned to them for help against his domestic foes. It was because of those links that Henry II dared not allow his subjects to establish an independent Norman state in Ireland. The interaction of Irish and British politics, arising naturally from geographical circumstances, thus introduced into the population of Ireland a distinctive element that persisted century after century and whose characteristic outlook was inherited by later groups of settlers.

This population rapidly became an integral part of the country's life; and there is no sound reason for regarding it as less than truly Irish. Ireland, after all, has no aboriginal inhabitants. All Irishmen, in every part of the country, are descended from invaders, conquerors and settlers; and no layer of settlement has any exclusive claim to be regarded as 'the Irish people'. It was, however, to assert such a claim that the term 'Anglo-Irish' was brought into use in the later nineteenth century: only those of Gaelic descent were to be regarded as true Irishmen and the rest of the population must be kept in mind of its 'foreign' character. 'I was brought up to think myself Irish without question or qualification,' wrote Stephen Gwynn in the 1920s, 'but the new nationalism prefers to describe me and the like of me as Anglo-Irish.'* If there is in this a note of mild resentment it is hardly to be wondered at: Gwynn was, on his mother's side, a grandson of William Smith O'Brien; his father, a Church of Ireland clergyman, had made a distinguished contribution to the study of early Irish history; he himself was for many years a Home Rule member at Westminster. But he came of a Protestant 'settler' family; and this was

---

* S. Gwynn, *Experiences of a Literary Man* (London, 1926), p. 11.

enough to make him, in the eyes of Gaelic enthusiasts, something less than a genuine Irishman.

Yet this term 'Anglo-Irish', if we ignore the narrow-minded racialism that gives it currency, can serve a useful purpose. It provides a convenient means of distinguishing between the two main Irish traditions—Anglo-Irish and Gaelic Irish. Both are part and parcel of the life and history of Ireland, which cannot be fully understood if we ignore either. The powerful revival of the Gaelic tradition in the later nineteenth century and its partial triumph in the early twentieth have tempted some historians to see it as the only 'true' line of Irish development; and this interpretation has influenced even those who would not wholly accept it, so that the Anglo-Irish tradition is commonly regarded as foreign, and even hostile, to Ireland. This view receives some colour from the tenacity with which the Anglo-Irish themselves strove to maintain the links between Ireland and England. But their motives in doing so were Irish, not English. They regarded Ireland as their own country, and looked to England to support them in maintaining their hold upon it. They believed, also, that the connection with England was essential to Irish well-being. The arguments of Burke in the eighteenth century and of Carson in the twentieth are alike based upon the conviction that Ireland could not be separated from England without economic disaster.

In short, the Anglo-Irish were a product of the geographical situation of the British Isles; and their tradition embodied one view of what that situation meant for Ireland and for Ireland's relations with England. It was a view that a majority of their fellow-Irishmen rejected, though neither so consistently nor so continuously as nationalist mythology would suggest; and it was a view that suited their own interests. But it was essentially an Irish view, a view held by men whose lives were committed to Ireland and whose future, whether as individuals or as a community, was inextricably bound up with that of their country.

It was in the eighteenth century that the power of the Anglo-Irish reached its widest extension. Their dominance was now established in every part of the country and in all departments of life; and there did not seem to be any opposing force strong enough to make headway against them. It was in this century that they impressed their mark most deeply upon Ireland; and in this century, also, the arrogant self-confidence that was one of their characteristic traits showed itself most clearly. But after the parliamentary union their influence began to decline, though almost imperceptibly at first; and a little more than a hundred years later, with the establishment of the Irish Free State in 1922, they ceased to count in the politics of Ireland.

To the ardent Gaelic nationalist the Anglo-Irish were simply a colonial garrison, the agents of a foreign power, the apostles of a foreign culture. In his mind, they stood for conquest and confiscation, for penal laws and Protestant ascendancy; and their removal from the political scene was not so much a consequence as an integral part of the 'national victory', opening the way for the establishment of a Gaelic and Catholic state. This may have been a natural enough reaction to the past, or, rather, to that partisan version of the past in which so many Irishmen were brought up. But the political helplessness of the Anglo-Irish was to have important consequences for the future of Ireland. They, almost alone among Irishmen, had the maturity that comes from long experience of exercising power and bearing responsibility. They could accept the need for compromise and make allowance for the views of those who differed from them. In the Convention of 1917–18 they had boldly abandoned their own former position in the hope of establishing a framework within which Irishmen of all persuasions would be able to co-operate for the common good of their country. They had been foiled by the combined efforts of Ulster Unionists and Roman Catholic bishops; and the eventual settlement confirmed what they had most feared and striven hardest to avert, the partition of Ireland. Six Ulster counties, having between them a strong Protestant majority, remained part of the United Kingdom, though with a local parliament for purely domestic affairs; the rest of the country became a self-governing Dominion within the British Commonwealth of Nations.

By the early 1920s, indeed, partition was the only viable means of avoiding a destructive civil war of indefinite duration. But if it was to bring lasting tranquillity then people on both sides must either agree to remain apart on a basis of mutual respect and co-operation or else move peacefully towards union under a common government. Either course would require patience, understanding and a readiness to compromise. But the men now in charge, both North and South, were locked in the rigidity of doctrinaire politics. Even the few among them who were capable of taking a broader view were more afraid of alienating their own supporters than willing to conciliate their opponents. To begin with, at least, it was on the conduct of affairs in the Irish Free State that future developments most obviously depended; for the government in Dublin was confident that the Six-County area would shortly be brought under its control; and, even after these hopes had been disappointed, it continued to regard the extension of its own authority over the whole country as no more than a matter of time. Would its policy, framed with this development in mind, do anything to dispel the traditional fears of the Northern Protestants, or would it simply confirm them? The answer to this question would go far to determine the course of Irish history.

The Anglo-Irish, had they retained any effective political influence, might at this stage have done something to save Ireland from itself. They had suffered cruelly during the guerrilla warfare of the previous few years and they were uneasy about the provisions of the Treaty; but they quickly and frankly accepted the new régime. Within days of the signing of the Treaty the archbishop of Dublin had publicly proclaimed the loyalty of the Church of Ireland to the new Free State; and the Board of Trinity College, Dublin, urged the parliamentary representatives of the University to give the Treaty their support. Thus the two institutions in which the Anglo-Irish tradition was most clearly embodied spontaneously announced their readiness to abandon old affiliations and to play their part in making a new Ireland. If they had been allowed to do so in any decisive way they might, perhaps, have convinced the rulers of the Free State that the choice before them was one between fostering the unity of Ireland and confirming its division; that if they wished to build up an Irish nation as comprehensive as that envisaged by Wolfe Tone and Thomas Davis it must include, on equal terms, both Anglo-Irish and Northern Protestants as well as Roman Catholics; that to demand territorial unity while emphasizing cultural division was an irresponsibly dangerous policy. But the Anglo-Irish voice carried no weight; the politicians went their own way; and the new régime in the South was as markedly Roman Catholic and Gaelicizing as that in the North was Protestant.

The conditions in the two areas were, of course, in some ways very different. In Northern Ireland the Roman Catholics were numerous enough to maintain, for a time, a guerrilla war against the government; and this, together with the long tradition of sectarian conflict in the province, meant that the majority regarded them with constant suspicion and did what it could to exclude them from all positions of political or economic influence. In the Free State, the Protestants had at once accepted the new régime; and they were, in any case, too few and too scattered to offer any kind of threat. It was perfectly safe to treat their leaders with respect and welcome their co-operation. But their characteristic outlook was not allowed to influence public policy. With every year that passed it became more and more clear that the Roman Catholic and Gaelic tradition of the majority was to be absolutely dominant. When De

Valera, speaking as the head of the Dublin government, publicly identified Irish nationality with Roman Catholicism he was only giving formal expression to the principle on which the Free State had been governed since its inception; and, in this context, his statement that Ireland 'remains a Catholic nation' reads very much like a declaration of intent. This was in 1935; and his declaration took on an ominous significance for the Northern Protestants two years later, when a new constitution claimed for the Dublin government *de jure* authority over the Six-County area.

This continuing determination of successive governments in Dublin to extend their authority, by one means or another, over the whole country gives special importance to the fortunes of the Protestant population actually under their control—the people, that is, among whom the Anglo-Irish tradition still survived. When the Irish Free State was established they amounted to rather more than ten per cent of the total population, a proportion that had remained fairly constant for generations. By the 1940s it had sunk to less than six per cent; and the decline has continued, so that it seems not unlikely that before the end of the century Protestantism will be virtually extinct over the greater part of Ireland.

However this sudden and catastrophic decline is to be accounted for, it has had incalculable consequences for Ireland. The Anglo-Irish might have supplied a link between the opposing forces, North and South. Though they and the Ulster Unionists had parted company in the Convention, their common Protestantism still counted for much; and the sight of a strong, stable, confident and influential Protestant minority in the Free State would have gone far to allay the suspicious fears of the Protestants of Ulster. The actual picture was very different; and to many people it provided ample proof that those fears had been justified; that Home Rule did indeed mean Rome Rule; and that the system of government under which Protestantism was dying in the South would, if allowed to do so, produce the same effect in the North.

But the Anglo-Irish, though now stripped of political influence and dwindling, in all appearance, towards a painless extinction, still survive; and, while they survive, they may even yet be able to make a healing contribution to the tormented politics of their country. Their double experience, of power and the loss of power, has bred in them a wisdom and a breadth of outlook that Ireland needs and cannot find. They stand for comprehension, instead of uniformity; for a frank acceptance of the fact that Ireland and Great Britain have so much in common that total separation can be to the advantage of neither; for a grateful recognition of the debt that Ireland owes to the cultural influence of England. Perhaps their fellow-countrymen are not yet mature enough to learn the lessons they could teach. Perhaps it is already too late for such lessons to be effective. But even if the Anglo-Irish are to die without again playing a part in politics, their record will remain a major element in Ireland's past—the record of a proud people who ruled proudly, whose achievements in art and literature, in administration and war, belong to Ireland, a people who, even in the helplessness of their decline, could have offered their country-men a way forward towards a true and comprehensive Irish nationhood. In 1792 the United Irishman, William Drennan, wrote to a friend: 'The Catholics may save themselves, but it is the Protestants must save the nation.' The words are as true today as when they were written, and as little likely to be heeded.

Index

Abbey Theatre, 140
Agrarian agitation, 46, 82-3, 87, 92-4.
    See Landlords
America, 27, 50, 53, 83
Architecture, 44, 66-72
Armagh, 61, 71, 81, 127
Athboy, 38

Baginbun Head, 13
Baldwin, Richard, 65
Banagher, 40
Banim, John, 138
Banim, Michael, 138
Bargay Castle, 59
Barrington, Sir Jonah, 52-3, 74
Bath, 73
Belfast, 71-2
Beresford (family), 39
Beresford, John, 68
Beresford, Lord John George, 90
Berkeley, George, 44, 69, 80, 131, 143
Bernard, John Henry, 126-7, 128
Bindon, Francis, 76
Birmingham, George A., 119
Bligh, John, 38-9
Boyle (family), 39
Boyne, 42, 67
Breifne, 18
Brian Boru, 38, 99, 102
Bristol, 56
Brooke, Charlotte, 134-5
Brooke, Henry, 76, 134
Browne, Denis, 105
Bruce, Edward, 19
Bruce, Robert, 19
Burgh, Thomas, 67, 69
Burgh, Thomas de, 105
Burke, Edmund, views of, on Ireland,
    55-8; on British Empire, 56-8, 59, 88,
    106; Anglo-Irish characteristics of,
    143-4, 145-6; 44, 53, 80, 124, 131, 149
Burke, Ulick, 23
Bushe, Charles Kendal, 84
Bushe, William, 105

Butler, James, *see* Ormond
Butt, Isaac, 111-12, 113, 115, 135

Canterbury, 16, 109
Carleton, William, 136, 137, 138
Carson, Edward, 123-5, 149
Castle Chamber, Court of, 32
Castle, Richard, 67, 69
Castlehaven, James Touchet, 3rd earl of,
    37, 38
Castlereagh, Robert Stewart, Viscount,
    60, 61, 84
Castletown, 69
Catholic Emancipation, 57, 61, 85, 89, 97,
    99, 136, 137, 141
Caulfield, Hans, 105
Cavan, 76
Charlemont, James Caulfield, 4th viscount
    and 1st earl of, 78
Charles I, 29, 31, 36
Charles II, 11, 35, 39, 41
Church of Ireland, in 18th century, 73;
    Swift's view of, 25, 54; character and
    outlook of, in 19th century, 103-10; and
    the Treaty of 1921, 151. *See* Dis-
    establishment, Evangelical movement
Clanrickard, 23
Clare, 40
Clare, Richard de, 14, 16, 22
Collooney, 70
Commons, House of, Old English in, 31,
    32; composition of, in 1661, 38-40;
    character of, in 18th century, 47, 48, 49,
    50, 64; and parliamentary union, 60-1,
    84; 9, 10, 52, 56. *See* Parliament
Commonwealth, 34, 35, 42
Connaught, 14, 16, 31, 64, 90
Connemara, 108
Conolly, William, 65, 69, 70
Conservative party, 112, 115, 116, 117,
    118, 120, 124, 126
Constitution of 1782, 50-1, 52
Convention (1917-18), 125-8, 129, 150,
    152